To dear Joyce
and Dr. Wilbur

With love -
Anna D. Mow

Your Experience
and the Bible

Your Experience and the Bible

ANNA B. MOW

HARPER & ROW, PUBLISHERS
New York, Evanston,
San Francisco, London

FIRST EDITION

Designed by C. Linda Dingler

Library of Congress Cataloging in Publication Data

Mow, Anna B
   Your experience and the Bible.
   Bibliography: p.
   1. Christian life. I. Title.
BV4501.2.M63   248'.4   73–6321
ISBN 0–06–066033–3

To my dear friend in the Lord, Eugenia Price, whose growth in the reality of Christ Jesus continues to inspire and challenge me

Not a MIRAGE which is:

On the desert—an optical illusion of
water to the thirsty.

In the darkness—a false light.

For my people have committed two
evils: they have forsaken me, the
fountain of living waters, and hewed out
cisterns for themselves, broken cisterns,
that can hold no water. *Jeremiah 2:13.*

But REALITY:

The mirage becomes a pool, the thirsty
land a bubbling spring. *Isaiah 35:7,* NEB.

Jesus stood up and proclaimed, If any
one thirst, let him come to me and
drink. He who believes in me, as the
scripture has said, "Out of his heart shall
flow rivers of living water." *John 7:37–38.*

I am the light of the world; he who
follows me will not walk in darkness, but
will have the light of life. *John 8:12.*

Contents

Preface

A young minister asked, "What would you say if I told you I am very much interested in Zen Buddhism?" I answered, "I have been interested in Zen Buddhism for years, but have you heard about the Holy Spirit?"

A stranger looking through American papers and magazines could easily come to the conclusion that the main faith of America is astrology. Even church people are bewildered about who and what God is or isn't. Many interpret God horizontally—in human relationships only.

To the surprise of many in this scientific age, everyone seems to want a religious experience. There is a deep yearning for, and curiosity about, the supernatural, but most people think an experience of faith is a *feeling*. This is an era of emphasis on feeling. But when even "good" feelings vacillate or disappear, they feel lost and wonder if there is any inner security anywhere.

This book is about how one may *know* when a religious experience is reality or merely a mirage. No one wants to be duped.

I believe the Bible can show us the way because it is the story of God reaching out for relationship with man. Of course, the Bible people were citizens of other lands, other eras, other cultures. No matter, we can profit by seeing how God, the same God, reached through to them in their own time, in their own circumstances, in the midst of their own cultures. Because people are *people* the ages through and the world around, we can learn from their experiences. With all the differences of time and culture we are looking to the same God.

I am ever grateful to dear Cecile Dowdy for her faithful typing and to Genie Price and to Clayton Carlson and John Shopp, my editors at Harper & Row, for their discerning suggestions.

ANNA B. MOW

Roanoke, Virginia

1 Our Need for God

Too many people do not know what Christianity is meant to be. The genuine has too often been replaced by the simulated. Even some jewelry is *guaranteed* to be *simulated* diamonds!

When my husband and I returned to America from religious India, I had to face the fact that to be religious even in the church does not necessarily mean that one is a Christian. The only difference may be that the "Christian" uses the name of Jesus instead of Allah or Krishna. The similarity can be in the use of religion and its forms rather than in any life-giving relationship.

I remember the lovely Moslem girl in Chicago who had earned a doctorate at the University. One day after she had delivered a lecture before a large secular audience, she was asked, "What surprised you most when you came to America?" I am sure the questioner was thinking of American gadgets and conveniences. But Zubeda answered, "Do you really want to know? Well, I'll tell you! You do all your religion on Sunday and there is no sign of it during the week." A Moslem or Hindu has a religion that relates to all of life. Religion permeates all daily activities. We, as Christians, must have more than "Sunday religion" before we can profess anything unique in our faith.

Perhaps this is what the honest, searching youth of this generation are rebelling against. Perhaps they want to know a real God of love who loves all people. We must ask ourselves, has the institutional Christian church truly represented such a God? Recently a Jewish rabbi said to several ministers, "If the man Jesus returned, he would feel more at home in my temple than in your churches." The question then: Is the church truly the Body of Christ?

In the early days of this century rationalists looked forward to a religionless society in which education and science would usher in a new world. Their hopes for this new world were blighted by the anxiety and insecurity which followed the second World War. With grasping hope people turned to the church, and its membership rose to its highest peak and remained there for the decade which followed. But church membership and togetherness weren't enough. Being religious did not necessarily mean a new relationship with God.

No wonder that a disillusionment with increased anxiety and fear came upon the people seeking a reality that would hold. The whole world knows that science has put into the hands of man the power to destroy the earth in a matter of minutes. The determining factor is no longer the tool in human hands but the emotional control of man in himself. The refrain in newspaper crime stories seems to be "I couldn't help it." The basic practical question is: Can the human being in this condition find the remedy for emotional helplessness?

Those who did not discover a real experience of God through their church life became indifferent and dropped the church. In this time of unprecedented fear and anxiety they do not know where to turn. Ministers and priests face discouragement. Methods and doctrines do not hold their people. One discouraged minister wrote to me. The first page of his letter was about "the people, *they*. . . ." He had not yet found them as individual persons. His second page was the complaint that in seminary he was taught all the answers to questions people never ask. But his third page held the crux of the matter: he needed a real personal experience of God himself. This minister saw the real cause of indifference, discouragement, and failure: the need for every person to know God in a personal way.

In spite of the fact that people are turning from the church, the evidence is that they are more religious than ever before!

The religiosity of America is front page news. *Harper's* magazine's feature article for July 1971 by Sara Davidson was the result of four months' research. She saw it as the "Rush for Instant Salvation."

There is a movement easing across the land, a movement in which individuals are trying to work out personal salvation—a way to proceed through life with harmony and peace, a minimum of tension, and a maximum of fulfillment. What we are witnessing is the flowering of a generation of seekers, a generation whose world boundaries were shattered by drugs, politics, street-fighting, encounters, communes, or rapid social change, and who came to believe in the possibility of an answer, a key that would make life better immediately. . . . How indeed, is one to judge the legitimacy of or find a sane path through the exotic salvation techniques?

One of Miss Davidson's conclusions seems to be that "the search becomes, in itself, the salvation"—but experience has proved that this is not the secret of salvation.

It has been said that people have lost their faith in the old beliefs, that they are refugees from the church. Many are turning to the stars for guidance, since they have lost faith in the God who created the stars. Instead of looking for new meanings in Christian faith, many are turning to everything but Christianity—even to such movements as the church of Satan whose creed is self-centeredness and participation in the "seven deadly sins." Next to the church of Satan is the popular revival of witchcraft. (Shades of the prophets of ancient Israel!)

Charles Reich in *The Greening of America* said we can understand better what is happening to the youth of America when we look at the style and values they reject:

It is that the goals of status, a position in the hierarchy, security, money, possessions, power, respect and honor are not merely wrong, but they are unreal. A person whose life is one long ego trip or power trip has not merely chosen one kind of satisfaction in preference to others; he has chosen goals that have no real relationship to personal growth, satisfaction, or happiness.

Reich recognizes that there should be a change in life style and values and then he asks: "How is changing one's way of life different from Christianity, which has failed over and over again for two thousand years?" Reich has not heard the kind of sermons I have heard, nor seen the kind of Christianity I have seen. I wish he had related another general statement to Christianity: "Because of the substitute phenomenon one of the prime characteristics of American culture is that the genuine is replaced by the simulated." The simulated may pass for diamonds, for butter, but when it comes to religion, why take an imitation or a substitute when the real experience of God is available for the asking?

Dr. Paul Tournier of Geneva, Switzerland, said at an Adventure of Living Conference in Portugal (which was reported in the December 1971 issue of "Faith at Work"):

Today, more than ever before, men are asking the question, "What is the meaning of life?" . . . What is on trial today is not religion as such, but the conventional religious life as we know it. What is it, we must ask ourselves, that is breaking down in the collapse of our world? It is anything and everything that is not authentic that is falling apart, everything that is appearance and not reality. . . . The whole civilization of appearances is thus being judged. . . . The problem is how to rebuild our world.

One of the great failures of some church leaders has been that they were like the "leader" who said, "There go the people. I must follow them, for am I not their leader?" Such "leaders" have taken their cue from what they think the people *want* instead of discerning their real inner needs and desires. It is like the teen-ager who said to me, "I wish my mother would tell me what time I had to come home. I wouldn't like it and I would rebel but I wish she would tell me anyway."

Young preachers have been told for some years to go out on

the street and meet the people where they are, even to join them. One of the funniest things I have read for a long time was an editorial in the Chicago *Sun-Times* for July 31, 1971. The theologians and academicians went out on the street one day to meet the people where they are. This time they encountered some "Jesus people," and they were baffled when the Jesus people asked them, "Do you know that Jesus loves you?" Their adjusted secular talk was no longer relevant. It was the young people who used the God-talk. Meet the people where they are! Indeed! Is even the church ready to meet them when they say "Jesus loves you"?

Not all "Jesus people" are "street people." Hundreds of them whom I have met are university students preparing to be doctors, psychologists, lawyers, teachers. It is as if they had been facing a wall full of sockets. Socket after socket was dead until they plugged into the Jesus socket—and it was *alive*. I shall not forget the radiance of the new-found joy of the university girl who exclaimed as she passed me, "I've just known Jesus for two months. Isn't He wonderful?" I was in her university four months later and this same joy was growing steadily in her life.

Many of these new Christians (*Christ*-ians) are not against the institutional church, but they are not always made to feel at home there. Laura is a college girl who is also a real Jesus girl. In a sermonette one Sunday she read I Corinthians 13 and, being practical, she said she had to practice it on her family first. Her answer to critics was in part:

You've seen young people and their "fads," haven't you? Well, have you ever seen a fad come to stay? Then open your eyes! The Jesus *movement* is here—and here it will stay. It's not only here, it is sweeping the whole country. And what could be better? Whether you think Jesus Christ to be Lord or lunatic, whichever, He surely has done a lot of good in this world. He's my Lord, let Him be yours!

Of course new converts are enthusiastic, of course young people are exuberant, but they are starting at the right place and with the right Person, Jesus Christ. Older Christians are responsible to stand by them and help them to grow in the new life. The church in Germany failed the "million youth for peace and a new world" after the first World War when it closed its doors to their meetings. We do not want Jesus to weep over us as He did over Jerusalem: "Would that even today you knew the things that make for peace!" (Luke 19:42).

Many other people today are traveling toward spiritual illusions. They don't know *yet* that there is no water for their thirst in that seeming oasis of hope, for it is a mirage. Those who have found the living water must recognize the thirst of all seekers without undue condemnation. They should wait in love by the wayside ready to give directions to the well that never runs dry.

Others are on the way, but possibly not according to an accepted pattern. They must be helped on the Way. I wonder if blunting the courage of an honest seeker isn't one of the greatest sins. Jesus met each person where he was and helped him into real truth. He kept people coming toward Him and never pushed anyone away.

He knows how much we all need Him, and He never fails in meeting that need when we look to Him.

2 Faith's Response to God's Outreach

In February 1948 I was scheduled to speak before a missionary group in Chicago. They had asked me to speak about Mahatma Gandhi. Before the day arrived Gandhi was shot at evening prayer (January 30) and all the world was talking about this man who wanted an experience of God more than anything else in life. Just before I was introduced one of the women whispered to me, "Do you think Gandhi went to heaven?" She was afraid I would call him a Christian even though he had never united with any organized church. At that moment I was called to the platform.

I began my speech: "I have just been asked if Mahatma Gandhi went to heaven when he died. My first comment is that it is not my decision to make. The second thing is that if he got there, I am sure he would feel at home because he loved the Lord Jesus and His teachings. I know many Christians who would not feel at home in heaven if they saw certain other people there. Third, if Gandhi got there he had the surprise of his life: all his life on earth he thought finding God depended on the intensity of his own search. If he got there he would find that God was reaching out to him all the time and wanting him even more than he wanted God. He would also find that God not only gave us an ideal in Christ, but that through the Holy Spirit He gives grace and power to be new persons in Christ."

It is strange that many Christians, even theological graduates, do not realize this basic spiritual fact revealed all through the Bible: *God takes the initiative* toward man. God took the initiative in the Creation of man. He reached out to him in his innocent state, and when man misused his gift of choice, God still came to him in his sin.

Years passed and the real God was forgotten, but people continued to be religious. Their imaginations conceived all kinds of gods and their hands even made them. But now man was taking the initiative in his relation to his gods, often to avoid retribution.

The Bible story of men who again really knew God begins with Abraham. (Gen. 12.) According to Jewish legends, Terah, Abraham's father, made idols and sold them in his own shop. They lived in the area of the city of Ur in Mesopotamia (now Iraq) which was the center for worship of the moon god, Sin. We wonder how Abram (so called at first) could come out of such a home and such a culture to become a man of faith in one personal God and then to become known even to this day as the father of the faithful.

Perhaps there is more than legend in this story out of Jewish "history." It is said that as a boy Abram loved the outdoors, especially at night. From a cave facing east he would watch the stars fade and the sun rise. He learned the dependability of the sun, moon, and stars. The stars must have meant the most to him because God spoke to him later in terms of the stars. He must have developed a sense of worship and reverence which he never had before the idols his father made.

The story I like best, told in Joseph Gaer's *The Lore of the Old Testament,* is about Abram when he was left in his father's absence to tend the shop. Whenever he was left in the shop he never sold anything. Perhaps he spoke to every customer as he did to an old woman one day. She came in to buy an idol to protect her from thieves. She said the thieves had stolen her other one. Abram said to her, "How do you think another idol can protect you when the last one failed to do so?" Ignoring his remark, the woman chose the one she wanted. Abram asked, "How old are you?" The woman answered, "Sixty." Then Abram said, "My father made that idol three weeks ago. How do you think it can protect you?" Then Abram took a big stick and began to break the idols all around the shop. In the meantime, the woman fled in fright. When Abram came to the biggest idol in the corner, he put the stick in the hand of the idol —and awaited the return of his father! His father, shocked to see all the destruction, demanded, "Son, what has happened here?" Abram answered, "The big idol got angry and knocked out all the little idols."

Such a legend might easily have had a basis in fact because Abram was ready to hear the voice of God. Something in him was prepared to respond in faith to this God whom he had not known about before. A listening ear had to be trained. His appreciation of the grandeur of the heavens had evidently quieted his soul so he could hear something from beyond earth's noises. When everyone including his own father worshiped idols, there must have been some reason Abram was ready to hear and to believe in an unseen God. If you have trouble believing in God, when even theologians say He is dead, you will know how remarkable it was for Abram to come to such a conviction. How Abram could come to such a faith intrigues me almost more than anything else about him.

In all the worship of that day the virtue and the efficiency of the worship depended on the initiative of the worshiper. How did Abram know to turn this around, to *"hear"* a "voice"—to recognize it as from outside himself—to be assured of a Presence so clearly he could stake his whole future on it? And seemingly he never gauged his faith by the condition of his feelings at any time.

When his father, Terah, left Ur, we do not know whether he was seeking new security or whether he merely had the sense of adventure which his son seemed to have. Anyway, he followed the route of other pilgrims and settled in Haran, another city of the moon god. It was here that Abram heard the voice of God, telling him to leave his country, his kindred, and his father's house and to go where God would lead him. "By faith Abraham obeyed when he was called to go out to a place which

he was to receive as an inheritance; and he went out, not knowing where he was to go" (Heb. 11:8). He also heard the promise
that he would be the progenitor of a great nation even though
he was now seventy-five years old and had no children!

Some modern scholars have called Abram a hobo, but that
term does not give the proper impression of this man at all. The
fact is that he was a rich family man. It is true he did not know
where he was going, but he did know whom he was following.
(Gen. 12:1–9.)

When Abram with his caravan came to Shechem, the Lord
appeared to him and said, "To your descendants I will give this
land" (Gen. 12:7). I don't know how God appeared to him, but
I know that Abram knew who spoke and what was said. He built
an altar there, as he did many other places later, and each place
he "called on the name of the Lord." We would say he prayed.
In each time of crisis he received assurance from God. God's
promise was renewed again when he had to separate from his
nephew, Lot. He had one unfortunate experience in Egypt
when his business sense and his cultural pattern overcame his
faith, but he returned to his land and his faith again.

The years passed and every birthday became a test of faith for
Abram. What about that promise of descendants? Besides all
that, in that day childlessness was a sign of the gods' disfavor and
Abram was jealous for his one God. His wife, Sarai, apparently
did not have her own experience of faith, and she had difficulty
going on her husband's faith. She was tired of the stigma of
childlessness, so she gave Hagar her handmaid to Abram to bear
a child for her according to the custom of the country. Abram
unfortunately listened to his wife's plan because the years of
waiting were becoming hard for him to understand.

When Ishmael, Hagar's son, was thirteen, God appeared to
Abram again. (Gen. 17:1–18.) There was no doubt in Abram's
mind about the communication. God reconfirmed his covenant
with Abram and as a sign changed his name to Abraham (Father
of a multitude) and changed Sarai's name to Sarah—and Sarah
was to have a son by Abraham! Abram, now Abraham, could not

help but laugh. He fell on his face and said to *himself,* "Shall a child be born to a man who is a hundred years old? Shall Sarah, who is ninety years old, bear a child?" Then Abraham said to *God,* "O that Ishmael might live in thy sight!" God said, "No, but Sarah your wife shall bear you a son, and you shall call his name Isaac." Then God appeared to Abraham by the oaks of Mamre through three men. They were entertained royally as any guest would be in that day. After a sumptuous feast the men asked for Sarah. She was eavesdropping at the tent door. When Abraham was told again that Sarah would have a child, Sarah laughed to herself, but the guests knew. They asked a wonderful question: "Is anything too hard for the Lord?"

Nothing *was* too hard for the Lord. Sarah did bear a son in due time and Abraham called his name Isaac. Only someone who knows the East can fully understand what it meant to Sarah to have her reproach taken from her. Having her own son as heir, she couldn't stand to have her Isaac playing with her servant Hagar's son, so she tried to get rid of Hagar.

The father-son relationship between Abraham and Isaac must have been remarkable. The years of waiting with promises only, the hopes through an adopted son blasted, their own contrivance for a son by the servant girl rejected by God—all these seeming disappointments only made the miracle of Isaac the greater. Fathers of that day held their hopes for the future in the oldest son. Sons in that culture honored their fathers. Abraham was a man to be honored and Isaac was a well-dispositioned person from all we know of him. So nothing in all of Abraham's life tested his faith so much as the test that was coming to him.

All around Abraham the people who worshiped idols followed a barbarous custom: when they felt bound to make the supreme sacrifice to their gods, they would sacrifice the oldest son for whom they carried their highest hopes. Abraham saw all this. Did he love his son more than he loved his God? He knew God was asking him this question. Abraham had to prove his faith.

One morning he rose early, took his son, two servants, wood, fire, and a knife. They walked and walked. Imagine Abraham's thoughts as they journeyed! On the third day Abraham left the servants with the donkey and told them to wait until he and Isaac returned. (Or would he return alone!) Isaac carried the wood and Abraham carried the fire and the knife as they climbed up the mountain together. At last Isaac broke the silence: "My father!" Abraham must have known what was coming, but he answered only, "Here am I, my son." Then Isaac asked the dreaded question, "Behold, the fire and the wood; but where is the lamb for the burnt offering?" Abraham could answer only in the area of his faith, "God will provide himself the lamb for a burnt offering, my son." The story says, "So they went both of them together."

If this had been a Canaanite father and son, the father would have been beating his breast and pulling his hair until he was drugged by suffering, for in his normal mind he would never be able to destroy his son. The chances are that he would have drugged his son also. But Abraham and Isaac walked up the mountain *quietly* together. This is one of the greatest differences between real worship of God and sincere obedience to Him in contrast with other kinds of religious experience. The man who knows God *waits on him,* but the pagan worshiper must take his own desperate initiative toward his god.

The obedience of Isaac and his honor for his father are underscored as he lets his father put him on the altar and bind him there. Did he not cry out in protest? I don't know. He may have been too shocked to speak because he had never seen his father do a cruel deed. Did they still hope that God would intervene? God did. As Abraham lifted his knife to strike his son, a voice said, "Abraham, Abraham!" No Canaanite father would have been in a mental state to hear *any voice* at that stage, but Abraham in the silence of his soul could hear. He answered, "Here am I." What glad words he heard: "Do not lay your hand on the lad or do anything to him; for now I know that you fear God, seeing you have not withheld your son, your only son, from me." Then Abraham lifted his eyes and saw a ram in the thicket, which he caught and sacrificed instead of his son. Abraham called the name of that place "the Lord will provide." Again the Lord renewed his covenant with Abraham, repeating His promises for him and his descendants. So Abraham and Isaac went back to the servants waiting on the mountainside and together they all returned to Beersheba.

No other man of Abraham's day had faith such as his. God reached through to him *in Abraham's own time*, in his own circumstances, in the midst of a culture alien to his faith. The miracle is that he could hold to his amazing faith in a living God who made promises without ever getting lost in the promises! He maintained his faith relationship to the God who called him, who made a covenant with him and gave him a commission to be a blessing to all peoples. From this time on it was God's plan to reach all people. Centuries later Paul could say, "Abraham believed God, and it was reckoned to him as righteousness . . . he grew strong in his faith as he gave glory to God, fully convinced that God was able to do what he had promised" (Rom. 4:3, 20–21).

The Biblical account of Abraham's faith is something beyond the senses, but it was not a "sixth sense." His faith seems to have begun out of his reverential awe of nature, but it was not centered in any *feeling* he got out of the wonder of nature. We never get the intimation that he was *trying* to have faith as so many people do today. His faith was not *contrived* faith, it was a *response* faith. It was not a result of intellectual deduction but came in the thick of his daily life. His response to a Personal God gave him an inner quietness that made obedience a spontaneous pattern of his life. His failures were not disobedience but overdependence on his own judgment without waiting to know better.

We are surrounded by a great cloud of witnesses that Abraham never knew. We should be so much more mature in our faith even though we are surrounded by much subtler idolatries. Paul said covetousness is idolatry. (Col. 3:5.) In fact, any thing, any position, any prestige, any person dearer to us than God is idolatry. Any unfocused person will find it difficult to have full faith in God. Faith begins by focusing on God—with faith that He *is*.

Many contemporary sophisticated minds say that God is no longer a useful hypothesis. The discrepancy may be in the word "useful." Too many Christians give the impression that they are trying to *use* God. Abraham did not come to faith by that road. I never had any doubts about my faith until after seven years as a missionary in India. After knowing and loving people of other faiths who had a great measure of peace in their lives, who were more "religious," I asked, "What do we have that they do not have?" I had to find an answer to this question for myself. My husband and I were at the University of Chicago in 1931 and 1932 while my husband studied Islamics. I needed help. Finally, I asked Charles M. Gilkey, Dean of the Chapel, for an appointment. I did not want to waste his time so I thought carefully about how to ask my question in the best way. I did much better than I knew then; I asked, "Just how personal is God?" Actually, this was the real question. Dr. Gilkey shared many things out of his own experience, also the humanistic conclusions of some of his friends at that time, then as he grabbed the arms of his chair, he exclaimed, "But I can never let go of the personality of God!" His own assurance set me free.

Religious people through the centuries have sought gods—or a God—but their anxious efforts stirred so much dust that they could not see the God who was seeking them. If God could get through to Abraham in his day, He can find us today if we do not get in our own way. I heard the great Martin Buber say, "God comes in whenever He is let in."

Behold, I stand at the door and knock; if any one hears my voice and opens the door, I will come in to him and eat with him, and he with me.

Revelation 3:20

3 Faith Tested by Difficulties

Generations came and went and a multitude of people called Abraham father, but they did not look like a people of the promise. They were in slavery in Egypt. But Abraham's God had not forgotten His promise. God's only problem was the people who forgot Him. The people needed a leader and God was preparing one.

Baby Moses was saved by his devout family, was nursed and taught in the royal household by his own mother and educated as an Egyptian prince. After he was grown he found out about the burdens of his own people. One day Moses caught an Egyptian beating a Hebrew slave. He knocked him down and accidentally killed him, then fled for his life into the desert.

In the rugged country of Midian Moses sat down by a well. Soon seven young women came to draw water. Some rough shepherds chased them away and used the drawn water for their own flocks. Again Moses was compassionate. He helped the young women and then saw them home safely. Their father was Jethro, a priest, who accepted Moses into his family and later as a son-in-law.

The desert provided much silence, the kind that makes or breaks a man. It strengthened Moses, and he learned to listen to silence. One day he saw a bush flaming, but it didn't burn up. Moses ran to investigate. Then God called to him out of the bush, "Moses, Moses!" He answered, "Here am I." The Lord said, "Do not come near; put off your shoes from your feet, for the place on which you are standing is holy ground. . . . I am the God of your father, the God of Abraham, the God of Isaac, and the God of Jacob." Moses recognized the voice as God's and was afraid to look. If this experience had ended there, Moses would have had a wonderful "testimony" to give of having heard the voice of God, but the God of the Bible does not stop with His Presence only, when He calls to man. He comes to enlist the called man in a cooperative effort in His concern for people who need His love.

So the call came to Moses: "I have seen the affliction of my people who are in Egypt, and have heard their cry because of their taskmasters; I know their sufferings, and I have come down to deliver them out of the hand of the Egyptians, and to bring them up out of that land to a good and broad land. . . . And now, behold, the cry of the people of Israel has come to me, and I have seen the oppression with which the Egyptians oppress them. *Come, I will send you to Pharaoh that you may bring forth my people,* the sons of Israel, out of Egypt." (Exod. 3:-1–17.)

Moses was reluctant to go because he was conscious of his inadequacies. Hadn't he also seen the oppression of the people and hadn't he tried to do something about it? Even though he was a member of the royal household, the king himself sought to kill him and Moses had to flee for his life. He had failed once. Why try again? Why would Pharaoh listen to *him?* Then God told him that the Pharaoh who had sought his life was dead, and God promised to be with him to meet the new Pharaoh. But what about the Hebrew people? They did not accept his efforts before; would they listen to him even if he told them the God of their fathers had sent him? They might ask, "What is his name?" God told him, "Say this to the people of Israel, 'I AM has sent me to you.' "

Moses' final excuse was his speech difficulty. The Lord answered him, "Who has made man's mouth? . . . Is it not I?" The Lord met Moses in his weakness and sent his brother Aaron with him to be his spokesman.

So Moses with his family and his brother went to Egypt, and Aaron told the people all the things which the Lord had told Moses. The people believed the message and they worshiped God. It wasn't long before Moses could not wait for Aaron to speak, but picked right up to do his own speaking for the Lord. He forgot his inadequacies after he got under the burden with the Lord.

After winning the support of the Hebrews, a slave people, Moses and Aaron still faced the fearful power of the whole Egyptian system. Could the God of Israel possibly be stronger than the military and political power of this formidable enemy? Moses and Aaron began with the faith that their God *was* stronger, but they were relatively new in this faith about the power of God, so at times they lost courage. (Exod. 5:22–6:9.) One day Moses cried to God, "O Lord, why hast thou done evil to this people? Why didst thou ever send me? For since I came to Pharaoh to speak in thy name, he has done evil to this people, and thou hast not delivered thy people at all." At least in such moments of discouragement *Moses turned to the Lord,* and each time he received assurance to continue in the way God directed. His sense of partnership with God was a miracle.

In this crisis God spoke to Moses again: "I am the Lord. I appeared to Abraham, Isaac, and Jacob as God Almighty. But I did not let myself be known to them by my name Jehovah. Moreover, I made a covenant with them to give them Canaan, the land where they settled for a time as foreigners. And now I have heard the groaning of the Israelites, enslaved by the Egyptians, and I have called my covenant to mind." Moses told the people again about God's promise of freedom and of their return to Canaan. He also gave this message from God: "I will adopt you as my people, and I will become your God. . . . I will lead you to the land." (Exod. 6:2–13, NEB.)

After many exciting difficulties Moses finally got the people free and out into the wilderness. But this was not the end of their troubles. Many times Moses must have felt that trouble had just begun. A slave people, they were unprepared for freedom, were actually afraid of it, and often longed for the security of slavery! They were not ready to meet the enemies in the land to which they were going. They needed inner discipline. They needed a wilderness experience as Moses had needed it, but they didn't *like* it! Nevertheless, the people were brought into an experience of a definite religious faith, a definite law, and a definite worship. Even though they still lacked maturity, a group of rebellious slaves was about to be forged into a covenant people under God, the God of Abraham, Isaac, Jacob, and now of Moses.

The greatest experience in the wilderness was the event at Mt. Sinai which Moses only seemed to understand. The people had been told many times never to worship any other gods, but they were slow to learn. (Exod. 20:1–3.) They wanted the security in worship of something they could see.

Moses went up on the mount for a special time with God. While he was gone the Hebrews took things in their own hands. "When the *people* saw that Moses was long in coming down the mountain, the *people* gathered round *Aaron*, saying, 'Come on, make us some god to go in front of us; as for this Moses, the man who brought us out of the land of Egypt, we don't know what has become of him!' " This suggestion was from the *spokesman of the people* who had no vision. Since Moses had shared so much with Aaron, Aaron should have had better insight and understanding, better sense than the people had, but he let the people manipulate him.

"Aaron said to them, 'Break off the golden earrings from the ears of your wives and sons and daughters, and bring them to me.' So the people all broke off their earrings and handed them to Aaron, who took and carved them with a tool into a metal calf." (Aaron didn't do that in a few minutes!) "The *people* cried, 'Here is your God, O Israel, who brought you out of the land of Egypt!' At this, *Aaron* erected an altar in front of the calf and proclaimed a festival next day for the Eternal."* (What a

*I understand that before Dr. Moffatt died he said he would prefer to say *the Lord* instead of *the Eternal*. I like that better.

compromise for a supposed leader!) "So next morning the people rose and offered burnt-offerings and brought recompense-offerings; then the people sat down to the sacrificial feast, *after which they rose to amuse themselves.*" (Exod. 32:1–6, Moffatt.)

After worship *"they rose to amuse themselves."* This is the evidence of false worship: it is self-centered, they wanted a religious experience which they could feel and touch. They were not mature enough yet for faith. And in this instance, shortsighted Aaron thought he had to follow the people in order to be their leader. Whenever I hear of a "way-out" program in a church I ask, "Who planned it, the youth or their leaders?" In every instance so far it has been the "leaders" who thought they had to do what they *thought* the youth wanted.

Moses came down from the mountain in great despair when he saw what Aaron and the people had done, so he asked Aaron (Exod. 32:21–24, Moffatt), "What did this people do to you, that you have let them incur great guilt?" Aaron answered his brother, "Let not my lord's anger blaze; you know how determined the people are to do wrong. They told me to make gods for them, to go in front of them, crying, 'As for this Moses, the man who brought us out of the land of Egypt, we don't know what has become of him!' I told them to break off any gold they possessed, and they gave it to me; I just threw it into the fire, and out came this calf!" (Ha!)

This was the greatest difficulty Moses had yet faced. His faith in the power of God and the call that had come to him had weathered all the threats of the power of Egypt, he had seen the complaining multitudes provided with food and water in the desert, he had heard the people promise, "All the words which the Lord has spoken we will do," after they heard the ten commandments and other words from the Lord, but now his own brother had let himself be manipulated by the people so that he let them commit this great sin.

All that Moses could do was to go back to the Lord and pray for these shortsighted, rebellious people. So he returned to the mount alone with God to pray for them. And what a prayer!

"Ah, this people has committed a great sin, making a golden god for themselves! Yet, wilt thou not forgive their sin? If thou wilt not, then pray blot me out of thy list of the living." What a picture of involvement and identification of a real leader with his people! Then the Lord practically told Moses that forgiveness and punishment were His prerogative. Was Moses trying to carry God's share of the load? Moses' part was to continue to follow the Lord's guidance: "However, go and lead the people where I have told you, and my angel shall go in front of you." (Exod. 32:31–34, Moffatt.)

Anyone called to a position of leadership today can learn much from Moses. His life was all drama, even in the monotony of the wilderness years, for he needed those years to balance the turmoil of others. He was born into a slave family, raised and educated as a royal prince, lived through years of exile, and then experienced the definite call from God to deliver a people out of slavery. His task turned out to be sociological as well as spiritual. A people with a slave mentality had to be led into the dignity of nationhood. Few of them were devout Hebrews who remembered about their father Abraham. The majority were more familiar with the gods of Egypt. In the face of all difficulties Moses never turned from the God who called him. He served as a leader in partnership with God. His religious experience was *God* and difficulties could not change that relationship. They only deepened it.

4   Faith Confronted and Confirmed

One of the most dramatic stories in the Old Testament is the contest on Mt. Carmel between the God of Israel and the gods of the fertility cult of Baal. It was set up by the prophet Elijah, often called the gadfly prophet. He would appear out of the nowhere and disappear as suddenly as he had come. He appeared as a rugged mountaineer in the midst of the elite culture that Jezebel, the Sidonian princess, brought with her when she married Ahab, the king of Israel. Jezebel was the women's liberation champion of her day who brought her idolatry and prophets with her. Ahab was putty in her hands. He built a temple especially for her worship and supported her eight hundred and fifty prophets out of the public treasury.

Rain needed for the farmers' crops was supposedly in the realm of the power of Jezebel's god, Baal. The prophet Elijah challenged this power. He strode into cultured Israel, wearing a garment of haircloth and a leather girdle, and announced to King Ahab, "As the Lord the God of Israel lives, before whom I stand, there shall be neither dew nor rain these years, except by my word" (II Kings 17:1). Then Elijah disappeared as suddenly as he had come and proceeded to hide himself east of the Jordan until the streams would go dry. Then the Lord sent him to dwell in Jezebel's home territory in the home of a widow to whom he was a great blessing. The inference of this move, of course, was that God was in control there also—in a "foreign" land.

In the third year of the drought the Lord said to Elijah, "Go, show yourself to Ahab; and I will send rain upon the earth" (I Kings 18:1). Elijah did not hesitate to go at the Lord's command even though he knew that Ahab had been seeking everywhere to find him in order to take his life. On his way to King Ahab, Elijah met Obadiah, a friend of God's prophets, whom Ahab had sent out to find water and grass to save his cattle. Obadiah exclaimed, "Is it you, my lord Elijah?" And Elijah answered, "It is I. Go, tell your lord, 'Behold, Elijah is here.' " Obadiah was deeply frightened, knowing his own life was at stake if he reported Elijah's presence and Elijah failed to appear. Finally, with Elijah's promise, Obadiah was willing to risk it. He reported, and Ahab went to meet Elijah. When he saw the prophet of God, he said, "Is it you, you troubler of Israel?" Elijah answered, "I have not troubled Israel; but you have, and your father's house, because you have forsaken the commandments of the Lord and followed the Baals."

Elijah proposed a contest on Mt. Carmel between Baal and the Lord. Elijah alone would stand in for the Lord, and four hundred and fifty prophets of Baal would stand in for their gods. Hosts of Israelites came to see the contest. Elijah said to them, "How long will you go limping with two different opinions? If the Lord is God, follow him; but if Baal, then follow him." It took faith in the living God to make such a challenge. The people listened. Elijah continued, "I, even I only, am left a prophet of the Lord; but Baal's prophets are four hundred and fifty men." The challenge was made, whichever god answered by fire for the altars should be accepted as the real God.

Elijah offered first chance to the prophets of Baal. They prepared their altar and the animal for the sacrifice. From morning until noon they called on their god, crying, "O Baal, answer us!" They danced frantically around their altar, beating their breasts, but nothing happened. "Elijah mocked them, saying, 'Cry aloud, for he is a god; either he is musing, or he has gone aside, or he is on a journey, or perhaps he is asleep and must be

awakened.' " So the Baal priests cried louder "and cut themselves . . . with swords and lances, until the blood gushed out."
This was their customary practice—to work themselves up into
an ecstasy in order to get response from their gods. "They raved
on until the time of the offering of the oblation, but there was
no voice; no one answered, no one heeded." No fire fell and no
rain came. The prophets of Baal had to admit defeat.

Then Elijah called all the people to him while he prepared
his altar to the Lord. Strangest of all, he asked the people to soak
all the wood on the altar with water. Then he prayed, "O Lord,
God of Abraham, Isaac, and Israel, let it be known this day that
thou art God in Israel, and that I am thy servant, and that I have
done all these things at thy word. Answer me, O Lord, answer
me, that this people may know that thou, O Lord, art God, and
that thou hast turned their hearts back." In a moment the fire
of the Lord fell and consumed everything including the stones
and the water! When all the people saw this, they touched their
faces to the ground and cried out, "The Lord, he is God; the
Lord, he is God." So the victory was won for the Lord, God of
Israel.

Then Elijah told King Ahab to hurry home because the rains
were coming. The drought was over.

The great contrast in the confrontation on Mt. Carmel was
not in the fact of one prophet of God in a contest with hundreds
of Baal prophets, it was not in the different methods used in
preparing the altars—the real difference lay between pagan
religion in prayer and a man of God in prayer. The pagan
prophets had to mutilate themselves and use all their energy to
beg their gods because they thought *their god's response depended on their own initiative and effort.* With all that effort
they received no reply. But the man of God was only respond-
ing to the prior outreach of his God. His actions and his requests
were even guided by God so he could wait in *quietness and
faith* for God to hear him and to answer. The true God did hear.
The fire fell and the rains came.

After such a wonderful victory for God over the gods of Baal and the response of the people in a new allegiance to the real God, Elijah should have been full of joy and thanksgiving—but he wasn't. There were those priests, still living! Why didn't God kill them off, he wondered, and make the victory complete? This time Elijah *did not wait* for guidance from God. *All his quietness disappeared.* Elijah was naturally a man of action, but on the mountain his fever to act hastily had been tempered by *waiting for God to act.* There he was *God-conscious.* But the sight of those priests turned him into a fire-breathing activist. The victory *for* the Lord wasn't enough now for Elijah; he wanted victory *over* the priests of Baal also. His spiritual courage had deteriorated into angry retaliation. From their hours of self-immolation the priests of Baal were greatly weakened, and they had no strength left to defend themselves. Elijah ordered the people to seize the helpless men; then "Elijah brought them down to the brook Kishon, and killed them there." To put it mildly, that was a bloody ordeal! Human nature being what it is—then as well as now—there wasn't much left of Elijah's quiet consciousness of a Holy God who had heard his prayer on top of the mountain that very day.

I don't know what Jezebel could have said if the God-victory on the mount had been the full story, but when Ahab told her what Elijah had done to her prophet-priests, she was understandably furious and sent a messenger to Elijah, saying, "So may the gods do to me, and more also, if I do not make your life as the life of one of them by this time tomorrow" (I Kings 19:2). Elijah fled for his life.

All of my young life this story bothered me. Why should fearless Elijah suddenly be afraid . . . of a woman . . . even Jezebel? I was never satisfied until I thought through what had actually happened to Elijah spiritually. Anyone so sensitive to God's spirit that he could go through the pregnant quietness of his faith in God up on the mount would naturally be disturbed by the gruesome experience of murder immediately following, whether he had a "reasonable theological" explanation for it or not. This was truly a letdown in faith even though we cannot blame him because of spiritual truths he had still not perceived. (Jesus had not yet come!) So now, I am sure, Elijah really did not run away from Jezebel, he *tried to run away from himself.*

After weeks of hiding in a wilderness cave on Mt. Horeb the word of the Lord came to Elijah again: "What are you doing here, Elijah?" Elijah was still full of self-pity and self-defense. He answered the Lord, "I have been very jealous for the Lord, the God of hosts; for the people of Israel have forsaken thy covenant, thrown down thy altars, and slain thy prophets with the sword; and I, even I only, am left; and they seek my life, to take it away." Had Elijah so quickly forgotten the victory for the Lord on Mt. Carmel and the response of the people to that victory? He had not yet faced what *he* had done. He remembered only what Jezebel had said and done. Then the Lord said to him, "Go forth, stand upon the mount before the Lord." The voice of the Lord had quieted him so Elijah was again ready to listen to God.

The prophet waited. "A great and strong wind rent the mountains, and broke in pieces the rocks before the Lord, but *the Lord was not in the wind;* and after the wind an earthquake, but *the Lord was not in the earthquake;* and after the earthquake a fire, but *the Lord was not in the fire;* and after the fire a *still small voice.* " (I Kings 19:9–13.) When Elijah heard the still small voice, or the *voice of a gentle stillness* (Hebrew meaning), he "went out and stood at the entrance of the cave" and again God spoke to him. God was in the voice of gentle stillness and spiritually Elijah was back where he had been on Mt. Carmel—in holy quietness before his God.

Discouragement and fear were now gone from Elijah as God sent him to give a message of calamity to Jezebel and Ahab. Hope for the future was given to him because God told him to anoint new kings for Syria and Israel and a prophet who would succeed him.

Elijah not only had faith in the God of Israel over all other gods, but in the return of quietness to his soul, he found reconfirmation of his own relationship to God.

Elijah has taken his place in the literature of the world as a great man of God. The New Testament refers to him more than to any other prophet. He appeared out of the "somewhere" to represent the prophets as Moses represented the Law when Jesus was transfigured on the Mount. By that time Elijah *knew* what he never knew on earth: the full wonder of God.

5 Reality Discerned and Misunderstood

*The idea of one who loves truth and justice but whose love is greater
even than his justice, the idea that man must find his goal by becoming
fully human, was carried on by men of vision—the prophets. Their
teachings became increasingly impressive because history bore them
out. Secular power which reached its peak under Solomon, collapsed
after a few centuries, never to be restored in an impressive way. History
vindicated those who spoke the truth, not those who held power.*
Erich Fromm, *You Shall Be As Gods*

From the day of Elijah to the end of the Old Testament
period the story of God's people is told through their prophets
and not through their political history. Only a few of the kings
were faithful to God. Wealth, prestige, power, and pleasure
possessed king and people alike. Religion was made to be a
handmaid to selfish interests. The people remembered the
words of the covenant repeated through the generations but
forgot the commission that accompanied it. As today, urbaniza-
tion increased the contrast between rich and poor. Those in
power exploited the downtrodden and the helpless. The nation
no longer lived as "the people of God." It is a marvel in that
time of spiritual deterioration that anyone could see clearly
enough to discern the will of God for His chosen people. But in
spite of all the religious confusion there was always a continuity
of prophethood in Israel and Judah.

The prophets saw God as the God of all nations and therefore not the private God of the "sons of Abraham" to be used by them for their special privilege. They would never be "saved" just because of their heritage. This was religious heresy to the "orthodox" religious establishment.

But even more flagrant was the prophets' discerning message that God was the God of all of life—that He expected religion to have a consistent bearing on all social life, in all business transactions, and in all political life. This was especially pertinent to Israel, because they were established as a "nation under God." A prophet who dared to expose the sins of the establishment was quickly accused of treason. He carried the burden of being misunderstood as God was misunderstood. As now, the true prophet who was "spokesman" for God was bound to live a lonely and dangerous life.

It always was and still is a temptation to separate the religious from the social, professional, and political affairs of life. Long before Jesus came, the prophets saw that "spirituality" divorced from daily life is no longer an authentic experience of God. Such "spirituality" becomes merely a mirage, a false hope.

Through the centuries when men have gone to the Bible for encouragement in their struggles for liberation of the underprivileged, they have found real inspiration in the message which Amos received from God and then wrote down because the people would not listen to him. In the 1940s someone rewrote the Book of Amos as if the prophet had proclaimed it on the corner of State and Madison Streets in Chicago. The message is as relevant as that for our day. It sounds like the cry of the youth who see the phoniness of many present day values in government, business, social life, and religion.

The message of Amos was as rugged as the life he had lived as a herdsman in his native Tekoa. In the quiet of the countryside he had developed a keen listening ear for God. He knew the Scriptures, the story of his people and their God. He may have sold wool in Samaria and Bethel. At least he knew of the unprecedented prosperity of the North—their luxury and self-indulgence gained through injustice and oppression. Amos saw the emptiness and farce of their religious worship. He knew that the religious prostitution which they practiced could not be a part of the worship of a Holy God. With all he saw, the prophet Amos was sure of one thing: corruption spells the doom of any people. So he warned them of the doom to come, challenging them to honest faith in God. No wonder a self-satisfied, proud priest sent him home!

Amos saw also that they were trying to *use* God by buying God's favor with their worship rituals. And if their festivals included religious prostitution, what of that? Didn't God create sex? Amos insisted that authentic worship brings the desire to do right and that no ritual is a substitute for merciful deeds. As he warned them of doom he also told of the great mercy of God for those who repent. But the people did not listen to Amos; they discredited him before the king who ordered him to stay on his farm down south.

Amos put ethics back into religion, he faced the poverty problem, the housing problem, establishment power in religion and state. He was as modern as a recent magazine headline, "Can Wall Street Afford a Social Conscience?" (*Saturday Review*, August 28, 1972.) He was misunderstood and unappreciated by the very people God had sent him to help, but disappointment did not break his relationship to God.

Hosea was the next man God sent to Israel. The doom Amos had foreseen was already coming to pass. Hosea was of the North and had a personal concern for his people and his nation. Revolt, anarchy, and bloodshed in the nation broke his heart. Increasing tragedies did not bring the people to repentance. Religion became even more corrupt. Highway robbery and organized vice were actually directed by the priests. Fear and uncertainty gripped the people. Family life had gone to pieces. Temple prostitutes were always available to men "worshipers." Men even found their own wives taking part in temple prostitution.

Hosea had discernment as keen as that of Amos, but with it

all he had developed an underlying tenderness for which he is called the prophet of love.

Hosea had come into a new understanding of the love of God that had never yet been discerned by other prophets, but he had paid a price for that knowledge in his own love story. Naturally a tenderhearted man, Hosea had fallen in love with a beautiful woman whom he married. They had three children. His wife, Gomer, had the same problem many women still have, the famous "problem that has no name." She grew restless with her life at home and finally ran away with another man. Time passed, but Hosea never ceased to love her and to long for her. Then one day when he was downtown he was shocked to see Gomer in a wretched condition and—up for sale on the slave market—a discarded woman, but not by Hosea. In spite of all her sin he bought her back and reinstated her in his home as his wife and as the mother of their children.

Then Hosea realized that if he could love Gomer after all that had happened, how much more must God love Israel who had also played the harlot. Hosea learned how love suffers, and he came into the realization that God also suffered when his chosen people failed him. Hosea found the balance between justice and love which deepened his understanding of God. He discovered that real strength is required for forgiveness. He could see that God was not minimizing sin because he could forgive a repentant people. To Hosea sin was unfaithfulness, but genuine repentance would bring forgiveness from the God who is love. No other nation had any idea of such a God of love. Even though Hosea did not live to see the people accept his message, he could trust in the hope and love of God who would be their Redeemer.

Isaiah is reckoned as the greatest of all the prophets. He knew that God is the hero of all Scripture, that it is God who determines the final outcome of history. With other prophets he realized that peace and true prosperity cannot be achieved except by living according to the will and plan of God. Isaiah recognized man's injustice as being against God even more than against man. At the time of his call he learned that people would not listen to his message, so he was prepared to face destruction and failure while at the same time he could preach hope because he believed in God. This faith in God was indelibly confirmed when he was called to be a prophet. Isaiah was also a statesman. He belonged to the court circle—the "establishment." He was well acquainted with kings and other high officials and knew their relationships with surrounding nations. He was well educated religiously and was devout in his worship of the Lord. So he was available when God needed him.

It was the year that King Uzziah died, a cataclysmic time in the nation. Isaiah was worshiping one day in the temple when the Lord appeared to him. Here is his story:

In the year that King Uzziah died I saw the Lord sitting upon a throne, high and lifted up; and his train filled the temple. Above him stood the seraphim; each had six wings: with two he covered his face, and with two he covered his feet, and with two he flew. And one called to another and said:

"Holy, holy, holy is the Lord of hosts;
the whole earth is full of his glory."

And the foundations of the thresholds shook at the voice of him who called, and the house was filled with smoke.

Isaiah 6:1–4

The most wonderful experience that can happen to anyone on earth is to come into such a consciousness of the living God. After an experience like that one can never be the same again. Life is indeed thrust onto another plane of consciousness. Then it becomes *natural* to think in terms of the kingdom of God and to be a real part of it by faith.

The first reaction to any vision of the holiness of God is never one of self-importance but of unworthiness. Isaiah cried out, "Woe is me! For I am lost; for I am a man of unclean lips, and

I dwell in midst of a people of unclean lips; for my eyes have seen the King, the Lord of hosts!" Then one of the seraphim flew to him and touched his lips with a burning coal from the altar and said to him, "Behold, this has touched your lips; your guilt is taken away, and your sin is forgiven." Then the voice of the Lord said, "Whom shall I send, and who will go for us?" Isaiah answered, "Here am I! Send me!" So the Lord sent Isaiah out with a message which the people would not like and which they would not accept.

Isaiah knew human nature well, he knew politics—the pull of power, the pressure of prestige, the appeal of pleasure; he saw how hard it had become for people in their sin of self-centeredness to turn to God. The only hope he could see was through some intervention by God's grace. He realized that they could expect no more than a remnant of the people to respond to God in humble faithfulness. But a remnant would be enough for a new start. He believed that God would send an anointed one, a Savior, a Messiah to help his people. A new age would come through God's grace.

Isaiah lived to see Jerusalem spared, but later the wickedness of the kings spoiled the work of God. It was Jeremiah who got the brunt of all the tragedies that followed the wake of Judah's disobedience to God.

Jeremiah was a priest, also of the aristocracy. He was brought up in the quiet company of scholars, priests, and students of the Scriptures. He also had a very definite experience of God in his call to become a prophet. The Lord told Jeremiah that he had chosen him to be a prophet even before he was born. Jeremiah hesitated because he was quite young and a poor speaker. Then the Lord said to him,

> Do not say, "I am only a youth";
> for to all to whom I send you you shall go,
> and whatever I command you you shall speak.

Be not afraid of them,
for I am with you to deliver you.

Jeremiah 1:7–8

Jeremiah indeed entered into the heartache of God as he spoke for the Lord the words concerning the spiritual condition of the people who had been a chosen people to serve and represent God:

For my people have committed two evils:
they have forsaken me,
the fountain of living waters,
and hewed out cisterns for themselves,
broken cisterns,
that can hold no water.

Jeremiah 2:13

As God's spokesman Jeremiah was constantly going against the current of his day. He had to cry out, "Why does the way of the wicked prosper? Why do all who are treacherous thrive?" (Jer. 12:1). Another time the Lord answered him, "Behold, I am the Lord, the God of all flesh; is anything too hard for me?" (Jer. 32:27).

With all his sufferings, even imprisonment for "treason," Jeremiah saw that the old covenant would not keep the people faithful. God would have to make a new covenant which would be an inner law: "I will put my law within them, and I will write it upon their hearts; and I will be their God, and they shall be my people" (Jer. 31:33). Jeremiah lived to see the best of his people led into captivity in 598 B.C., but he still had full faith in God. God still had mercy for His people even though they brought their captivity upon themselves.

Many faithful people were caught in the national tragedy. Ezekiel was one of them—another aristocrat who loved God. He had a great concern for his people. One day God came to him in a vision, and he heard a voice speaking. Ezekiel said,

"And when he spoke to me, the *Spirit entered* into me and set me upon my feet." Then he was given a message of hope. He was told to give the Lord's message whether the people listened or not. Usually they didn't listen. But at a most discouraging moment God gave Ezekiel the vision of the valley of dry bones (Ezek. 37). Old dry bones were scattered throughout the valley. *They were very dry.* Ezekiel was told to prophesy to the bones. He obeyed. And lo! there was a rattling sound, the bones came together, flesh came on them, and then breath came into them! Then the Lord said to Ezekiel, "Son of man, these bones are the whole house of Israel. . . . O my people, I will bring you into the land of Israel. And you shall know that I am the Lord. . . . I will put my Spirit within you, and you shall live. . . ."

From a human standpoint the "people of God" were in a hopeless situation. They had lost everything, and they had nothing in the land of their fathers to go back to. But those who knew God knew that there was hope. Out of this hope came a great expectancy. God gave them a promise, and they were sure something would happen. How would He do it?

After the return to the land of their fathers the Scriptures were gathered together and Israel became a people of the Book. Idolatry was no longer a temptation. In several centuries without any prophet receiving direct word from God they sought God's will in the Scriptures. But still, as now, the majority of the people forgot that they were to be priests for God and not His pets.

God was waiting.

The prophets waited with Him.

A few simple folk lived so close to God that *they* were ready for Him.

> In returning and rest you shall be saved;
> in quietness and in trust shall be your strength. . . .
> The Lord waits to be gracious to you.
>
> Isaiah 30:15, 18

For to us a child is born,
  to us a son is given;
and the government will be upon his shoulder,
  and his name will be called
"Wonderful Counselor, Mighty God,
  Everlasting Father, Prince of Peace."

Isaiah 9:6

6 Reality Revealed

For God has allowed us to know the secret of his plan, and it is this: he purposes in his sovereign will that all human history shall be consummated in Christ, that everything that exists in Heaven or earth shall find its perfection and fulfillment in him.

Ephesians 1:9, 10, Phillips

On December 31, 1971, the Associated Press reported that in that year Jesus had become the greatest hero on the American youth scene. Accepting Jesus as a hero is a good idea because we tend to become like our heroes. But Jesus as hero is only a good starting point. He is so much more than a hero. He is the revelation of what God is really like, He is Savior, and He is the revelation of what it means for man to be made in the image of God. He is also our example of perfect relationship with God and perfect experience of God. In Him we can find the difference between religious experience as such and a real experience of God. The present efforts to bring Jesus near to us by emphasizing His humanity are laudable, but the question centers on the definition of *humanness* as well as on the difference between His humanness and ours.

Some years ago I happened to be standing with three ministers as they were discussing their temptations and shortcomings. One of them said, "But after all, we are only human." I had an uneasy feeling about that statement until I realized that we must not *excuse* our failings because of being human, we must *confess* them so that we may grow out of them by God's grace.

In Nazareth of Galilee the wonder of the humanity of Jesus hit me hard. I never had any doubts about His divinity or deity but I realized then that His humanity was a miracle indeed. We need to be clear on what His humanness encompassed. Recently, many writers have included *weaknesses* in His humanity. It is one thing for youth just starting out with Jesus to do this; it is quite another matter when a theologian does it. I went through one book and crossed out most of the adjectives used to describe Jesus. I wondered what the author was trying to cover up or excuse.

I am less human when I *yield* to human temptation and frailty; I am more human when I let the Spirit of God help me to conquer irritation, discouragement, anger, and hate. Real humanity lies in fulfillment of personality, not in its frustration. Jesus was never less than we are, neither does *His* humanity excuse our weaknesses. It will never do to make Jesus an ordinary human *because He was not ordinary*. He was and is truly our Savior, able to help us to grow to full maturity in Him which is true maturity as a human being.

In teaching a class on "The Life and Teachings of Jesus" I discovered that there was no difference between His life and His teachings. He *was* what He taught. The first and most important fact of His life on this earth was His unquestioned commitment to the will of God. That was absolutely settled in His life. He had only one question to face: "What *is* my Father's will?"

This commitment to God was an experience of growing understanding in the human life of Jesus. We know so little about His childhood and young manhood, but we do have the story of His visit to the temple when He was twelve. He felt at home with the religious teachers there and loved talking with them about God. He even forgot his customary thoughtfulness and obedience to His parents and didn't notice when they left for home. When they returned after three days of searching for Him, they could not understand His answer to their anxiety:

"How is it that you sought me? Did you not know that I must be in my Father's house?" In His deepened religious consciousness Jesus did not rebel against His parents but was obedient to them. And He *"increased* in wisdom and in stature, and in favor with God and man." (Luke 2:49, 52.)

It was eighteen more years before Jesus felt the call to leave His home and the carpenter shop, but these were not wasted years. He was alert to the happenings and hopes of His day. His education in the synagogue was in the Scriptures. From the quotations he used later we know that he especially appreciated Deuteronomy and the prophets. Of the prophets He found the greatest kinship for His thought and purpose in the writings of Isaiah. He knew that through all the agonies of Israel's history they were still God's chosen people and that through divine intervention God would fulfill all his promises. He knew the theologies that had developed since the time of the prophets and all the interpretations concerning the promised Messiah. He was a craftsman and so he knew how to be one with the common people without any stigma of "paternalism." He loved nature and the things of the land and the sea. His later parables were remembered because they were of everyday life. Jesus also knew that God called no man merely to give him an experience, but that everyone was called to be a messenger and a blessing to all peoples. These were years of waiting on the Heavenly Father and growing in the oneness He already had with Him. Jesus *knew* God as a Father.

Then word came about the ministry of John the Baptist down south by the Jordan River. Jesus heard that even Jews were being baptized. (Before this only Gentiles were baptized when they converted to Judaism.) The people were pouring in from everywhere to hear John—common people, tax collectors, soldiers, and theologians. In no uncertain terms John told them where they were failing their God. It was a restless era and people wanted to hear the truth told straightforwardly. They listened to John with great interest and asked, "What shall we do?" He told them to repent and change their lives. They even asked John if he were the long-expected Messiah (Luke 3:15). He answered that he was not even worthy to untie the shoes of the one who was coming, that he was only a voice in the wilderness, making the paths straight for the coming of the Lord.

When Jesus came and asked for baptism, John knew enough to say, "I need to be baptized by you, and do you come to me?" Was it a surprise to John to find that he had actually baptized the Messiah? I only know that when they came up out of the water, as Jesus was in prayer, heaven opened, the Holy Spirit descended upon Jesus as a dove, and a voice came from heaven, saying, "Thou art my beloved Son; with thee I am well pleased" (Luke 3:21). What an experience for both men!

In the midst of the crowd that came to be baptized Jesus could have argued against His own need of baptism, but He was always guided by a deeper motivation than argument. I once had a teacher who often said, "The greatest evidence of the divinity of Jesus was His unerring instinct to do the right." The voice from heaven assured Him He was doing the right thing. After all, the main experience in baptism is the commitment of one's life to God. In His baptism Jesus not only identified Himself with the Father but also with all mankind. He was both Son of God and Son of Man.

All the convictions that had been developing in the quiet of His private life came to fruition as Jesus yielded to the baptism of John and received the full sanction of the heavenly Father. In the fullness of the Holy Spirit He was led by the Spirit into the wilderness to test out in final form the principles He was to work by in the ministry to which the Father called Him. He needed only to be sure of the Father's guidance, because He was already committed to that will. All His life He had heard theological interpretations about the coming Messiah. He was smack up against a fixed theology. Were His deepening discernments right? The struggle for clarity through the fog of His human limitation was so intense that for over a month He was not even conscious of hunger. But when the issues clarified, His answers were automatic because it was *already settled* that He would do God's will. He never had any struggle on that point.

As the tension of the struggle ceased His hunger returned, so, of course, the first temptation had to do with physical sustenance. Jesus was far from any food shop. With His new consciousness of Spirit power why shouldn't He turn those round flat stones into bread? Didn't God provide manna in the wilderness for the children of Israel? (Deut. 8:1–3.) The tempter's question was based on the premise, "If you are the Son of God!" Yes, why shouldn't He make bread for Himself by a miracle? But Jesus *knew* He could never use His spiritual power for Himself because that would break His identification with us. His answer was ready: "Man shall not live by bread alone, but by every word that proceeds from the mouth of God." There was another implication also. If He sought to win people by meeting their physical needs only, they might never come to a real spiritual hunger. They would then follow Him only to get out of Him what they could for themselves.

Later experience proved this discernment to be exactly right. You remember, after He fed the five thousand the people were so thrilled at the prospect of having a leader who could provide for all their physical needs that they attempted to make Jesus king. He was not fooled by their adulation—he knew the "quality" of such a following. He never cashed in on any publicity, but withdrew into the quiet of the hills. The people did not give up. When they found Him, He said to them, "You seek me . . . because you ate your fill of the loaves." Then He challenged them to seek the spiritual food "which endures to eternal life." He said His Father gives the true bread. They asked for this bread. He answered, "I am the bread of life; he who comes to me shall not hunger. . . ." The people were dissatisfied and said, "Is not this Jesus, the son of Joseph, whose father and mother we know?" (John 6:25–42.) So easily do the masses turn when they do not get what they think they want!

The people of Israel expected a conquering Messiah. Jesus had to face that expectation. Since the return from captivity many men had come proclaiming themselves the promised Messiah, but they all failed to free the people from foreign kings or the occupying army. The theologians expected the Messiah to restore the throne of David with all the past glories of Israel. The common people wanted relief from oppression. The temptation was to display power to win a following. Jesus had a power the self-proclaimed Messiahs never had. Wouldn't the people fall for Him if He would jump from the pinnacle of the temple and be saved by the angels as the Psalmist promised? He would not fail as other "Messiahs" had done if He could do that without harm. But Jesus saw through the tempter's scheme. "You shall not tempt the Lord your God." How clean this discernment was! It was proved true the first time He came back to His home town. The word had reached the homefolk about His miracles and good works in other places. They expected a display of this same power for their benefit, but He did not put on a show for them so they became angry with Him. They tried to put Him out of the city—His home city—by force, but He calmly walked away from them. Again the question came, "Is this not Joseph's son?"

The third issue that was clarified for Jesus during His temptation was concerning methods He would use to win followers. The devil asked Him to take the world's way, but Jesus recognized the subtley of this temptation and answered, "Be gone, Satan! for it is written, 'You shall worship the Lord your God and him only shall you serve.' "

The same temptation comes to us in other words: "Be practical. You know how the people are! Nothing but power works in this world. Get the people in any way you can—by any possible promotion scheme—and then teach them." Jesus did not accept the nationalistic "power-wielding Messiah" theory at all. His concept was illustrated as *salt, light, life, love.* Isaiah's concept of the suffering servant grew on Jesus as He faced the problems of His ministry. The common people and the "sinners" heard Him gladly. They knew their needs. It was people with vested interests, especially among the religious leaders, who made His way hard and who gave Him so much trouble.

When Jesus returned from the mount of temptation, He was set for a kind of ministry new to the world. His relationship to the heavenly Father was the most outstanding fact of His religious experience. In His own words, the basic reality of His experience was, "I and the Father are one" (John 10:30). "I can do nothing on my own authority; as I hear, I judge; and my judgment is just, because I seek not my own will but the will of him who sent me" (John 5:30). *The Fatherhood of God* was mentioned by the prophets, but it was more the fatherhood of a nation. Jesus took that name for God and made it His own— and ours by faith.

Jesus never lost sight of the majesty, justice, holiness, and vastness of God, but at the same time He revealed how near God can be in infinite gentleness and love. His prayer life was not a religious discipline, it was a dialogue in love with understanding and communion. No wonder His disciples asked that He teach them to pray. The disciples were praying men, but the prayer life of their Master was completely different from that which they had known. He taught them what we now know as "the Lord's Prayer." It has often been said it is really a disciple's prayer. But actually in one way it is truly the Lord's Prayer because it is the witness of His experience with the Father: God, tender Father, approachable, inviting, loving, and still the great Creator of all. It is the witness of His integrity of soul in reverence and worship: "Hallowed by Thy name." It is the witness of His own purpose in life followed without hesitation or compromise: *Thy will be done on earth as it is in heaven.*

Jesus had settled the relationship of spirituality to daily material things of this earth. His incarnation was not only a theological idea, it was a practical daily experience because He was revealing God's interest in, and love for, man. He was the embodiment of loving forgiveness even through the agony of the Cross, and we cannot be in Christ without that same forgiving spirit. So the prayer says *forgive us as we forgive.*

It is contrary to ordinary human nature to love one's enemies —even to love some neighbors—but Jesus was always talking about the possibility of a new nature. Even to theologian Nicodemus, one of the leaders of the church of that day, Jesus said, "You must be born again." In Christ the Spirit can make this kind of love natural and spontaneous.

One of the most creative and revolutionary experiences of the spiritual life of Jesus was His attitude toward sinners. Religious leaders of that day were very exclusive in their social contacts. They thought they would be defiled by such associations. But Jesus ate with sinners, loved them, and talked to them without condemnation. His own reputation was never at stake because He knew God loved all people. No wonder the despised of the earth crowded around Him. They had never been loved before.

What Jesus taught in the Sermon on the Mount was a real witness to His own experience of God as it worked out in His human relationships. We have seen His purity of heart or singleness of purpose and His passionate desire to do the will of His Father, we know He was a peacemaker and that He was persecuted for righteousness' sake, but so few Christians seem to know what He meant by *poor in spirit* or *meekness.* The world ridicules the "meek" even while it tries to walk over them. It thinks the meek stand *passively* before whatever happens to them, that they are without dignity or any positive spirit.

Jesus was meek, but He was *strong.* His reactions were never determined by what others did to Him. He had an unquestioned security in God and the assured dignity which sets one free to forget himself at the same time that he is "being himself." He was above the fear of competition or any need of *self*–defense. Paul understood this in Jesus: "Though he was in the form of God, he did not count equality with God a thing to be grasped, but emptied himself, taking the form of a servant. . . ." (Phil. 2:2–11.)

Without seeing the *strength* required to be meek as Jesus was, one cannot understand His "cleansing of the temple" experience. I do not believe He "lost his temper." Jesus was capable of deeper emotion than any other man and He could show this emotion without losing His poise. Every time He came to the temple from His boyhood days He must have felt deeply about those buyers and sellers in the house of prayer. They had "practical reasons" for being there, but also they were in the Court of the Gentiles, which would crowd out Gentiles who wanted to worship there. Mark says Jesus said, "My house shall be called a house of prayer for all nations" (Mark 11:17). He knew God loved everyone.

What Jesus did in the temple that day was not a sudden outburst. The hour of crisis had come for Him. The day before when He entered the city He entered with a heartbreak; He wept over the city with the prophet's cry, "You did not know the time of your visitation." (Luke 19:41–44.) If this had been merely an act of force, the people of the temple could have stopped Him. Why did they let Him get away with it? They knew they were in the wrong and now the true Spirit of God's house challenged them. They fled.

Jesus was popular with the common people, but opposition from the authorities was growing stronger and stronger. They watched Him constantly and set traps to find a case against Him. One wonders at His poise and assurance—that He could remain free to perform miracles and to teach under the gaze of critical, watching eyes at the edge of every crowd. So sure was He of the Father's will that He was unaffected by the growing antagonism.

But the consciousness of death was growing upon Him. He tried to warn His disciples, but they couldn't bear to think of such a thing. Even the three who saw His transfiguration on the Mount could not realize what it meant, but Jesus had the assurance of the Father's will. Again there was the Father's voice, "This is my beloved Son, with whom I am well pleased." I wonder how often Jesus read the 53rd chapter of Isaiah during those last days! So often our vision stops at the cross: "Looking to Jesus . . . *who for the joy that was set before him endured the cross* . . ." (Heb. 12:2). Jesus could take the suffering because the only purpose in His life was to do the Father's will, and he could take anything that happened to Him while doing the Father's will. He knew, as the prophets did, that God would have the last word.

When Jesus was being tried before Pilate, the people then thought Jesus was on trial, but after nineteen hundred years history says Pilate was on trial before Jesus. They did everything to Him that frustrated earthly power can do, but they couldn't get anything out of Him but love because that is all that was in Him. God *is* love. Jesus was the revelation of God's love to the end of His humanity. They killed Him—they thought. But love cannot be killed. God cannot be destroyed. The grave could not even hold the remains of His human body. He burst the bonds of death. The Christ was alive!

Estelle Carver, Jamaica's gift to the Christian world, said, "If I had been the risen Lord I think I might have been tempted to go to the Sanhedrin first to say, 'See who won!' " But Jesus was still in character, in fact He was never out of it, and He appeared only to those who knew Him before, and to everyone since then He is the available risen Lord.

Do you want to have a real experience of God, not just a religious feeling? You begin by accepting Jesus as Lord—with all that means for all relationships.

Before he left the earth Jesus made all necessary arrangements for us to have an experience of God. Hear Him.

7 Christ's Open Door to Real Experience

Jesus had called twelve men to be with Him, to learn how to follow, and how to lead others. They were a "small group" school. They had a treasurer but no secretary. Jesus did not require them to take notes because they would depend too much on the words He said, and He wanted them to become sensitive to the leading of the Holy Spirit as Jesus was. During the few years in which He was with them He emphasized the kingdom of God and what it is like, but the last night before His death He taught them about the Holy Spirit.

Once before He had given them a lesson on the Holy Spirit. It was in the temple at the time of the Feast of Tabernacles. This feast was one of three most important festivals of the Jewish year. Attendance was compulsory for all Jewish male adults within a radius of twenty miles of Jerusalem. It was a great occasion. Each day the people came, carrying palms and willows to the temple, and there they marched around the altar, forming a roof over the altar with the palms. A priest brought a quart of water in a golden pitcher from the pool of Siloam as the people recited: "With joy shall ye draw water out of the wells of salvation" (Isa. 12:3, KJV). Then the priest poured the water on the altar as the people sang their praises to God.

Jesus was over in the midst of the crowd—He had no credentials to serve at the altar. Jesus was always so relevant, I can imagine the rest of the scene. With the background of people rejoicing over God's gift of water the voice of Jesus rang out, "If any one thirst, let him come to me and drink. He who believes in me, as the scripture has said, 'Out of his heart shall flow rivers of living water.' " They did not understand what Jesus meant, but years later John explained, "Now this he said about the Spirit, which those who believed in him were to receive; for as yet the Spirit had not been given, because Jesus was not yet glorified." (John 7:37–39.) The Holy Spirit had always been present, but people had to know Jesus *as He revealed God* before they could be filled fully with His Spirit. John was saying that there was a coming of the Holy Spirit dated in history which would make possible the full reality of an experience of God.

The disciples had no thought of Jesus leaving them and were deaf to His repeated warnings. They were still rejoicing in being with their Master, the human Jesus. They still had the old theological idea that the Messiah would restore the kingdom to Israel and get rid of the Roman occupying army. But Jesus knew His hour had come.

It was Passover time. Jesus wanted a special meal with His disciples. He sent Peter and John out to prepare the meal for which Jesus had already made some arrangements. (Luke 22:- 7–13.) They must all have known that trouble was brewing. Judas had already planned to betray his Master. Was he trying to force the hand of his Lord into political action? Of course, Peter did not know what a test was coming for him. They still wondered who would have the chief seats in government when Jesus, their Messiah, conquered His enemies and the enemies of their nation. They didn't know at all—yet—what the crisis was really about.

While they were at the table together, Jesus arose and girded Himself with a towel; then, as a servant, He proceeded to wash the disciples' feet. They were appalled. When Jesus came to Peter, Peter would have none of it. He would never let his Master stoop to wash his feet! Jesus answered him, "If I do not wash you, you have no part in me." Peter's love answered, "Lord, not my feet only but also my hands and my head!" They were bewildered. Why should their Master take a servant role?

After Jesus again had taken His place at the table, He said to them, "Do you know what I have done to you? You call me Teacher and Lord; and you are right, for so I am. If I then, your Lord and Teacher, have washed your feet, you also ought to wash one another's feet. For I have given you an example, that you also should do as I have done to you. Truly, truly, I say to you, a servant is not greater than his master; nor is he who is sent greater than he who sent him. If you know these things, blessed are you if you do them." (John 13:1–17.)

This lesson of servanthood, with no fear whatever of being made a slave, is even to this day the hardest lesson for Christians to discern and to live. But it is an absolute requirement for the coming of the Holy Spirit. This kind of servanthood is the most positive, self-giving outreach to God and to others that anyone can have. There is nothing passive or weak in it.

Judas left the group, and then Jesus began His real teaching of the evening. The first important point was about love: "A new commandment I give to you, *that you love one another; even as I have loved you, that you also love one another.*" They were sure of His love, and now this same love was to be the test and witness of their discipleship.

Jesus spoke of leaving them. Where could He be going, and how could they know the way to where He was going? He said, *"I am the way, and the truth, and the life."* They couldn't understand. Much less did they appreciate then the blank check He gave them: that they could ask anything in His name and He would do it. Even more, He said that when He went to the Father, they would be able to do the works He had been doing—and even greater works. He had just talked to them about servanthood, and now He talked to them about the power they would have. They could not yet see the connection.

A comforting word which seemed out of place to the disciples then was *"I will not leave you desolate."* He said they would understand later what He meant and then to those who loved

Him He would reveal Himself. They would not be desolate because the Father was going to send the *Counselor, the Holy Spirit,* to them. This *Counselor would teach* them all things and would *bring to remembrance* all that Jesus had taught them. Centuries later this statement is still a comfort to us. Some people have said we cannot depend on what John wrote about these teachings of Jesus because he wrote them so many years later. But John did not write these things until they had been *lived* and truly tested by the disciples. This is much better than if John had made a tape recording that night in order to preserve the teachings of Jesus only as words.

Jesus told a parable of the Holy Spirit as *life,* a new life within. The Holy Spirit is more than an outside influence. He is new life within. In the parable of the inner spring (John 7:37) Jesus pictured the Holy Spirit as infinite resources from within; in this parable the Holy Spirit is the life itself. Everyone in Jesus' day knew about the grapevine and its branches. The branch cannot bear fruit of itself; it must be connected with the vine. Jesus said, "I am the vine, you are the branches. He who abides in me, and I in him, he it is that bears much fruit, for apart from me you can do nothing." (John 15:1–11.) We know that if a branch is merely tied on it will die. It must be connected. People wonder why their lives are barren and a bore. Perhaps they are only tied on.

Many have heard my own parable of our cotton poplar trees. They grew so fast that every other year the electric light company came to top them to keep the limbs away from the wires. Six years ago my husband asked them if they would like to cut the trees down so they would not have to come again to top them. They were delighted and were so kind as to cut the trunks into logs to fit our fireplace. My husband hauled the logs to the backyard. All spring and summer those crazy logs put out little limbs and leaves—they did not know they were dead! There are still a few logs left, but there is no question about their deadness now. Too many church people are living off of leftover life from home and church, then they wonder why they feel so dead. They really are—if they aren't connected to the source of life.

The disciples could not understand why Jesus would leave them, but He assured them, "I tell you the truth: *it is to your advantage* that I go away, for if I do not go away, the Counselor will not come to you; but if I go, I will send him to you." (John 16:4–11.)

We can understand that now. How thankful we should be that He is here in the Spirit rather than as a mere human being. He is no longer limited by humanity. People can have Him in Nazareth, Jerusalem, Chicago, Boston, and we can have Him just as truly wherever we are. It is indeed to our advantage that He did not remain in His physical body.

Jesus did leave those disciples, the Counselor did come, and He is *here now*. More than nineteen hundred years later, He is with us and others all around the world. Now we can know that the Holy Spirit is not a substitute for an absent Lord but the agent and mediator of His living Presence. *To be filled with the Holy Spirit is the same as to be filled with Christ.*

Jesus also told them, "I have yet many things to say to you, but you cannot bear them now." He knew the law of spiritual readiness. He was not condemning them because they did not understand everything He was teaching them. He had faith in the coming Holy Spirit: "When the Spirit of truth, comes *he will guide you* into all the truth." (John 16:12–13.) If Jesus had told them about future developments in the church, its organization, its sacraments and symbols, its social relations in a changing culture, the disciples would have been tied to a guide list of rules which they would have followed legalistically. But Jesus planned only for the Spirit as a guide through whom they would have continuous relationship with Him. They would continue to obey a Person whom they loved rather than a set of rules. Jesus said the Spirit will not speak on His own authority, but whatever He hears He will speak. *And whatever the Spirit does He will glorify Jesus.* Again the Spirit and Christ are one.

Before they parted that last night Jesus prayed for His disciples. "I do not pray that thou shouldst take them out of the world, but that thou shouldst keep them from the evil one." Then He added, "As thou didst send me into the world, so I have sent them into the world." Our pattern for relationship to the "world" is the same as we find in the life of Jesus. He always loved the sinner, but never his sin, and He always showed the way out of the sin without any discouraging condemnation of the sinner. We have been so slow to learn this. The temptation is to condemn the sinner or to minimize the sin. Love seems hard to come by—because we have failed to see the place of the Holy Spirit in our lives. Jesus meant all this for us in the twentieth century also. He prayed, "I do not pray for these only, but also for those who believe in me through their word." (John 17:15, 18, 20.) We are in their heritage.

Jesus went through that last night without any human fellowship, even though His disciples loved Him so dearly. During the worst of the suffering most of the disciples were scattered in their despair. Throughout the night Jesus took the worst that man can do to another—and much of it was done by the orthodox religious leaders of the faith! Dying on a cross was the greatest shame that could come to anyone in that day. We forget that too often when our symbols of the cross are so beautiful. For Jesus it was the endurance of shame and seeming defeat. All those who loved Jesus were in total despair.

Then came the third hopeless day—they thought. But it was the greatest day of all! The glorious news soon spread. Jesus was alive! He had risen from the dead. Then for forty days they would see Him and then He would as suddenly be gone. But they grew into the consciousness of His Presence whether they could see Him with their own eyes or not.

Just before He disappeared from their sight in the Ascension, He told them they were to return to Jerusalem and wait for God's promise to them, the baptism of the Holy Spirit. They thought that now the great hour had come, the kingdom would after all be restored to Israel. (It didn't happen until 1948!) Jesus practically told them that that was none of their business, that that was a political issue, and He was talking about something else. And that something else was really something! "But you shall receive power when the Holy Spirit has come upon you; and you shall be my witnesses in Jerusalem and in all Judea and Samaria and to the end of the earth." (Acts 1:3–11.)

Thus far Jesus had spoken of the Holy Spirit as an *inner spring of water* (infinite resources), *inner life*, and now He added the idea of *power*. The Greek word used here for power is the same word from which we get the words "dynamo," "dynamite," "dynamic."

As the disciples watched their beloved Master, He disappeared from their sight into a cloud. When He had disappeared in death, they were in despair, but now when He disappeared in life, they went back to Jerusalem *full of joy* to wait for the promise Jesus had made them. (Luke 24:52.) They went to the upper room of the home where they were staying. Besides the eleven there were many others, including the mother and brothers of Jesus. One hundred and twenty of them devoted themselves to prayer and praise.

In that upper room they waited *without* striving for any personal religious experience; they were not thinking about themselves at all, but about their Lord. They did not know *what* was going to happen, but they knew Jesus would keep His promise.

Many thoughts must have gone through their minds during those days of waiting. Did Peter in his own heart come to the place where he gave up all self-striving? Did he yield his impulsiveness? Did James and John give up all their desires for first place in the kingdom? Did Thomas surrender his doubts? A new humility must have grown in their waiting hearts. They grew in faith and love to the place where God could come to them with the new promised power. It takes preparation to handle power.

The day of Pentecost was a very important Jewish holiday.

There is always an air of expectancy before a big holiday. On this day for the friends of Jesus there was a double expectancy. *Then it happened!* A sound of heaven! It filled the house! A tongue of fire appeared on the head of each person present: disciples, laymen, women. They were all filled with the Holy Spirit and began to speak as the Spirit gave them utterance. The sound was so great the multitude outside heard and came together, and to their amazement each one could hear the disciples speaking in his own language. This was a miracle of communication, for the people were in Jerusalem from many language areas.

Peter was still the ready spokesman, but this time he got up *with the eleven*—not in competition with them. He preached the first sermon of the Christian Church. He quoted the prophecy of Joel concerning the promise of the Spirit (Joel 2:28–32), and with assurance he said, "This is it." They all *knew.* Peter could now speak of the death and resurrection of Jesus with an understanding he never had before: "Let all the house of Israel therefore know assuredly that God has made him both Lord and Christ, this Jesus whom you crucified" (Acts 2:36). This courageous statement made by the same, and yet not the same, Peter who only a few weeks before had denied any relationship with Jesus before a servant girl!

The Holy Spirit is given for witnessing and for service. Jesus had said that conviction of sin was the work of the Spirit. (John 16:8.) Most of our failures come when we usurp the work of the Spirit and try ourselves to bring conviction of sin to people. The Spirit did that work on Pentecost. The people cried out, "What shall we do?" Peter said, "Repent, and be baptized every one of you in the name of Jesus Christ for the forgiveness of your sins; and you shall receive the gift of the Holy Spirit. For the promise is to you and to your children and to all that are far off, every one whom the Lord calls to him." (That includes us right now.) Peter saw what many Christians today do not realize— that this gift of the Holy Spirit is a norm in the God experience for every Christian. That means it was not for the apostles only, nor for the people in the upper room only, nor for the people of that day only, but for all of us from that day to this who love the Lord Jesus Christ and become His fully committed followers.

Three thousand were baptized that very day. What would any church today of one hundred and twenty members do with three thousand converts in one day? To know what really happened on the day of Pentecost one must read the whole book of Acts—in one sitting, if possible. A new day had really come. They all entered a new world in which Christ was King and Lord and where a new fellowship of believers came into being.

8 Christian Reality in Community

The outward evidences and manifestations on the day of Pentecost were minor compared with the power released in the lives of otherwise insignificant people. The outward evidences were a joy to experience and to remember, but the new consciousness of the *Presence* in their lives and community was so wonderful that they understood now what Jesus meant when He said it was better for Him to leave so the Spirit could come. It took the whole book of Acts and the Letters of the New Testament to tell what had really happened on the day of Pentecost.

J. B. Phillips in *New Testament Christianity* reports the astounding change as recorded in the book of Acts:

The fresh air of Heaven blows gustily through these pages, and the sense that ordinary human life is continually open to the Spirit of God is very marked. There is not yet a dead hand of tradition; there is no over-organization to stifle initiative; there is neither security nor complacency to destroy sensitivity to the living God. The early church lived dangerously, but never before has such a handful of people exerted such widespread influence. There is courage to match the vision; there is a flexible willingness to match the divine leadership. And there is that unshakable certainty against which persecution, imprisonment and death prove quite powerless. To put it shortly and in the common phrase, the lasting excitement which follows the reading of this book is this: *The thing works!* What might have remained no more than a beautiful ideal is set to work in an actual human situation, and with truly astonishing impetus the Church moves forward on its way.

The disciples were now living on a new plane of consciousness. They were new people at home in a new power. This power was so real that it seemed they took its availability *for granted*—so great was their faith in the Holy Spirit. They were more conscious of this God-power than they were of themselves or their former weaknesses. They were indeed new people. Even though they continued in their former worship at the temple, they felt a real need for separate meetings of their own in Christ's name.

One might think that the original group of one hundred and twenty would have been swallowed up in the thousands who joined them, but the power and the love in their midst were great enough to encompass everyone. They felt no need—yet —to appoint a committee to work out a socioeconomic plan whereby they might live according to the principles of Jesus. They loved the Lord and one another and *wanted* to share. Spontaneously, those who had land and possessions sold all they had and put the proceeds into a common fund. There were to be no rich and no poor among them. They would be one in Christ. No orders had been given and no rules made. The community living was not the main miracle, the miracle was that the company of those who believed were of one mind and heart.

This community fellowship was so dynamic and so powerful that when Ananias and Sapphira tried to deceive the fellowship, they died in the attempt. They wanted credit for giving all to the common fund while they secretly kept some for themselves. Their sin was not that they kept part of the money but that they wanted everyone to think they had given it all as others had done. Their real sin was spiritual pride, but they were sensitive enough to the group consciousness that they could not sin against the group or God and live through it.

Too few church people have taken seriously enough the dynamic of the first Christian church. There has been too much dependence on gimmicks, schemes, or business plans for the development of the church. Of course, plans and organizations are necessary and important except when they are substitutes for the work of the Holy Spirit. In this day of desperate desire for reality, both spiritual and social, communes have become popular. But communes as such can also be a mere gimmick and a danger as an end in themselves.

The depersonalization of persons in a big corporation age makes individuals cry out desperately for life-meaning. For many people the small-group movement seemed to be an answer, but after twenty-five years of experimentation the movement as a fad is reaching an end. Just getting people together for short periods or even for life did not bring an answer. Perhaps it is time that the organized church at least should restudy the true dynamics of the early church.

After the first World War the church in Germany failed its new youth movement. We heard much in those days about "a million youth for peace and a new world." The church then was afraid of the movement and did not permit church buildings to be used for youth meetings. However, there was a Student Christian Movement secretary, Eberhard Arnold, who loved the Lord and young people, and he met with them. In their search for new ways of life one night they read the whole book of Acts. One youth suggested that they try living together. That was the beginning of the Bruderhof communities, known in America as the Society of Brothers. (See *Torches Together* by Emmy Arnold.)

For the past seventeen years our son Merrill has been with the Society of Brothers. Of course, that caused me to be sincerely interested. From the first I was satisfied on my two main concerns: was it Christ-centered and was it family-centered? Through the centuries many communal efforts were merely sociological in goal, even more were so ascetic that they had no room for families. Others included families, but the family was not a responsible central unit. I am so thankful our grandchildren in this community have the security of a family of their very own, but also the security of the love of the larger family of God.

After fifty years of growth, difficulties, and blessings, this group still testifies by their words and life that God lives, that He has a will for men, that He and His will are revealed in the life, death, and resurrection of Jesus of Nazareth, and that He makes His will known to all those who seek Him. This is their only goal and the sole reason for living in community. In this day of emphasis on worldly success they reject human honor and human authority in their life together. They are resolute in their purpose to avoid all manipulation of people, any use of pressure on others, all selfish ambition and social climbing, all class, caste, and hierarchical structure, all unfreedom and un-genuineness. I have often marveled at the sense of freedom each person has in the community.

If Christ sets a person free (Gal. 5:1), then any fellowship in His name should make this freedom possible. The training for this freedom in the Bruderhof in truth begins with the little children and continues through all their growing years. No-where else have I seen such definite training for the ability and responsibility to make individual choices. Of course, this includes the love discipline that every child needs for his own security and freedom, for no child is so insecure as the one who never knows how far he can go.

It is interesting—and tragic—to see how impossible it is for secular sociologists to understand what can happen in such a Christ-community. A number have tried, but they cannot fathom the workings of the Holy Spirit. How true it is that "the unspiritual man does not receive the gifts of the Spirit of God, for they are folly to him, and he is not able to understand them because they are spiritually discerned" (I Cor. 2:14).

In this day when people think everything they ever believed in has been shaken, I am often asked how I feel about the church. I always ask, "Which church do you mean, the institutional church or the Church which is the Body of Christ?" Then

I quote, "The things that are shaken are obviously things which can be shaken. They are thus revealed to be man-made, passing or temporal things by the very fact that they are shaken. And they are being removed out of the way so that the things which cannot be shaken may remain" (enlargement of Heb. 12:27, anon.). It is only the institutional church which looks shaky. It needs changes. But the powers of death will never prevail against the Church which is the Body of Christ.

With the phenomenal increase in the number of the early Christians, it became apparent that some kind of organization was necessary. The Hellenists, who were Jewish Christians with Grecian background, found that their widows were neglected in the daily distribution of food. The "twelve" called the body of disciples together and said, "It is not right that we should give up preaching the word of God to serve tables. Therefore, brethren, pick out from among you seven men of good repute, full of the Spirit and of wisdom, whom we may appoint to this duty. But we will devote ourselves to prayer and to the ministry of the word." (Acts 6:1–6.) This pleased the people, and no one saw anything wrong in the division of labor. At least they recognized that even "serving tables" required the power of the Spirit. The men of prayer and preaching had no prerogative on the work of the Spirit. So seven men full of faith and of the Holy Spirit were chosen for the distribution of food and other necessities.

One never knows what will happen when the Spirit is in control. The Spirit-filled church was not bound by this first effort at organization. The "twelve" were amenable to changing conditions and entirely responsive to the Spirit themselves. No one seems to have been disturbed because two of the appointed deacons became great preachers. Stephen became the first Christian martyr after he preached a sermon. Philip became such a great evangelist that for the rest of his life he was known as "Philip, the evangelist" and not "Philip, the deacon." Philip even had four daughters who were preachers.

The fellowship in the Lord of the first Christians kept them together in their joys and in their sufferings. They could all rejoice over the lame man healed at the Beautiful Gate of the temple. They rejoiced because Christ was praised. Then when Peter and John got thrown into jail, there was a fellowship of concern—with rejoicing. No argument could be found against the truth because the healed man was walking among the people. When Peter and John were released, they came at once to the praying fellowship. The group prayed only for more courage to speak the Name of Jesus. No wonder the wise teacher, Gamaliel, warned the authorities: "So in the present case I tell you, keep away from these men and let them alone; for if this plan or this undertaking is of men, it will fail; but if it is of God, you will not be able to overthrow them. You might even be found opposing God!" (Acts 5:33–42.)

A youth asked a very pertinent question: "Is the voice of the church the same as the voice of God?" It is easy to understand that when members of a fellowship love one another, they would be thoughtful of one another. But it is even more wonderful when they can be together as a group and be guided by the Spirit as a group. This really means unity in the Lord. This happened in the church at Antioch. One can expect wonderful things from a church started by the Holy Spirit.

The Christians were scattered everywhere after the persecution which followed the murder of Stephen. Most of those scattered preached to Jews wherever they went, but several men of Cyprus and Cyrene came to Antioch and preached to the Greeks. The Lord was with these men and many Greeks accepted the Lord. When the church at Jerusalem heard this they sent Barnabas to them. He was glad for what he found. Then Barnabas went to Tarsus where Saul had gone after his conversion. Barnabas brought Saul, and they ministered to this new church for a year. This is the place where the followers of Jesus were first called Christians.

This church was a Spirit-filled church, it was a missionary-minded church. They heard of famine in Jerusalem, so they sent relief with Barnabas and Saul. After they returned, the church had a season of fasting and prayer. During this worship the Holy Spirit said to the group, " 'Set apart for me Barnabas and Saul for the work to which I have called them.' Then after fasting and praying they laid their hands on them and sent them off. So, *being sent out by the Holy Spirit, they went. . . ."* (Acts 11:19–30; 13:1–4.)

God needs human cooperation in His church, but there is no substitute for the Holy Spirit.

9 Faith Tested by Cultural Change

In a time of change all truth is tested. Only that which is real can stand the test. Those who are spiritually committed to God and are intellectually honest will welcome such testing for the further development of their own faith. Those who are full of fear in times of change probably have their security in old ways rather than in the Lord, and they may find only husks and dead forms left. They too will dry up and become hard. There are others who jump into anything which is new just because it is new. They will find no stability or security because their structure is built on the sand.

The first Christians had to face a greater test than any have faced since then. As *Christian* ways were still developing, they had no precedent to follow. As people committed to God, they had only the Old Testament Scriptures for direction. They did not realize yet what changes would come because of the life, death, and resurrection of Jesus. Jesus had not told them that the Gentiles would want to join them in their fellowship and that later there would be more "Gentiles" than "Jews" in the Christian church. But He did tell them that the Holy Spirit would be the guide for their lives and actions. So all the future depended on their sensitivity to the guidance of the Spirit. They would be led in paths completely untrodden before. As we watch *them* finding their way through drastic changes, *we* can find a secret for ourselves in our times of transition.

It is true that God told Abraham to be a blessing to *all* peoples. It is true that this great truth was clear to many of the prophets, but it was not easy for even the "faithful" to remember this. It is so easy to find one's security in *ways* of thinking and *ways* of doing things. It is easy to be so grateful for blessings we receive from God that we tend to forget that we are called to be priests and not God's pets. To good Jews faithfulness had become a very exclusive experience. Jesus had told them that through the Holy Spirit they would be led into fresh paths. That day came. The Gentiles as well as the Hellenist Jews wanted to accept Christ. The earth-shaking question was: Must they become "Jews" first before they could be counted as Christians?

The new Christian community members continued their relationship to the temple and the synagogues. The Old Testament was still their only Scripture. They kept the Jewish Sabbath from Friday night to Saturday sundown, and then had Christian meetings on the first day of the week because that was the day Jesus arose from the dead. But the time had come when they had to decide what to keep of their religious customs and what to carry over from the Jewish community of faith to the Christian community of faith. They had to find out what *was* Christian. The Spirit brought on the crisis.

At Caesarea there was Cornelius, a centurion, who was a Roman officer of the occupying army in Israel. He was one of the many Gentiles who honored the Jewish faith, devoutly prayed to God, and gave liberally to the people. Cornelius was told in a vision that his prayers had been heard and that he was to send for one Simon who was called Peter. He was even given Peter's Joppa address. So Cornelius called three of his men and told them what had happened to him, then he sent them to Joppa to bring Peter. Cornelius and his men had reason for concern. Would Peter, a Jew, come to him, a Gentile? Even God-fearing Gentiles knew of Jewish traditions deeper than race. Would Peter, a Jew, feel compromised, even defiled ceremonially, by visiting a Gentile home?

All the Gentile Christians had been Jewish proselytes, so Peter had not yet faced the possibility of a Gentile becoming a Christian without *first* becoming a Jew. At the time Cornelius sent for Peter, Peter was staying with a tanner; and that was a step in the right direction, because tanning was an "unclean" job to a Jew. God still had a communication problem. Would the Holy Spirit get through to Peter to change his deepest religious-cultural convictions? Was Peter sensitive enough to the Spirit for him to be ready to accept the three Gentiles whom God was sending? The process of changing cultural patterns, especially religious ones, is slow and often traumatic. Peter came through this traumatic experience with greater insight into the love of God.

The three servants of Cornelius had forty miles to travel. Over every mile they must have wondered if Peter would return with them at the invitation of their honored master. They were nearing their destination when it was time for God to get Peter ready for the big surprise.

Peter had come into the house hungry. While food was being prepared he did what he loved to do: he went up on the housetop alone to pray. As he prayed he grew drowsy and fell into a trance in which he saw a sheet being lowered from heaven. In it were animals a Jew was not permitted to eat. Peter heard a voice, "Rise, Peter; kill and eat." Peter answered, "No, Lord; for I have never eaten anything that is common or unclean." The vision was repeated and the voice added, "What God has cleansed, you must not call common." When this happened the third time, poor Peter was truly perplexed as to what all this meant.

Meanwhile, the men from Cornelius were knocking at the door downstairs. While Peter was still on the housetop "pondering the vision, the Spirit said to him, 'Behold, three men are looking for you. Rise and go down, and accompany them without hesitation; for I have sent them.' " Of course, Peter did not know yet that the visitors were Gentiles. (Why should the Spirit tell him what he would soon find out for himself?) So he went down to meet the men, but he was not shocked when he saw that they were Gentiles because he was still more conscious of the vision he had just seen. He said most graciously, dispelling all their fears, "I am the one you are looking for; what is the reason for your coming?" They told him the story of God's visitation to their master, Cornelius, and extended his invitation to Peter.

Peter had never entertained Gentiles before, but he invited the men to come in and he kept them all night—a real breakthrough. The next morning, accompanied by some of the brethren, Peter went with his Gentile guests. When they reached Caesarea the next day, Peter found Cornelius waiting with a houseful of guests. Now, Cornelius didn't know anything about this man Peter, but any man introduced by an angel must be great, so he bowed down to worship him. Peter was shocked by this homage. He cried, "Stand up; I too am a man."

Then Cornelius stood up and told the story of his experience four days earlier, and added, "So I sent to you at once, and you have been kind enough to come. Now therefore we are all here present in the sight of God, to hear all that you have been commanded by the Lord." Peter gladly told the story of Jesus' life, death, resurrection, and His command to the disciples to go out to witness for Him. "While Peter was still saying this, the Holy Spirit fell on all who heard the word. And the believers from among the circumcised who came with Peter were amazed, because the gift of the Holy Spirit had been poured out even on the Gentiles. For they heard them speaking in tongues and extolling God." So Peter declared, "Can any one forbid water for baptizing these people who have received the Holy Spirit just as we have?" Then and there they were all baptized in the name of Jesus.

When Peter and the brethren got back to the home church in Jerusalem, they found that the news about the new converts had preceded them and, of course, the most conservative among the brethren criticized Peter for even going to the Gentiles! "Why did you go to the uncircumcised men and eat with them?" they asked. These sincere brethren were still living by the old rules and hadn't learned any better yet, but they turned out to be teachable. Peter explained everything that had happened, especially why he was sure he had followed the guidance of the Spirit, then he added, "Who was I that I could withstand God?" This silenced the critics and even they "glorified God, saying, 'Then to the Gentiles also God has granted repentence unto life.' " (Acts 10:1-48, 11:1-18.)

If Peter's vision had come to me, that sheet would have contained shrimp, raw oysters, raw fish, and Manila duck eggs. I would have enjoyed the ham in Peter's sheet! (You ask about the duck eggs? Put them in warm straw for nine days, then cook them. In Manila on every bus and even on the street people were eating those duck eggs when we were there for a fortnight in February 1940. They knew which end of the egg had the "juice." They tapped that end, drank the juice, then broke the shell and ate the embryo. You don't need to make a face! It is perfect food scientifically—but I never ate one. I was prejudiced.)

In spite of the fact that the early Christians *wanted* to be guided by the Spirit, their problem didn't settle itself very easily. But God was patient with them as He had been from the beginning of His relationship with man. He had His eyes on a certain Jew, Saul, who loved his God and was completely dedicated to Him even before he could accept Jesus as the Messiah. Some scholars think Saul had planned to be a Jewish missionary to make proselytes from among the Gentiles. (See *Paul* by Gunther Bornkamm.)

Saul's home atmosphere nurtured him in this dedication as a "Hebrew born of Hebrews" (Phil. 3:5). Tarsus, his home city, was the best and the worst of Hellenistic civilization. Saul's father was a Roman citizen, so Saul was born to this privilege also. In other words, Saul was a citizen of two worlds: a Jew of high standing and a privileged man in all of the Roman empire. In the midst of Hellenistic culture, however, he was always grateful that he was a Jew and that he was educated in Jerusalem as a devout Pharisee. To the Jews he was Saul, but to the Greeks and Romans he was Paul.

Saul heard about Jesus and His followers in Jerusalem. He

believed sincerely that they were wrong, that they had strayed from the true faith. He wanted more than anything else to do God's will—he needed no challenge to commitment, for that issue was settled in his life. So, how could God get across to this honest conscientious man that Jesus was truly the Messiah, the Son of God? God has more trouble with "saints" who have their theology inflexibly settled than with "out-and-out sinners." Argument won't reach them. God found a way to get Saul.

"Orthodox Saul" was fighting for his God. He stood by while "unorthodox Stephen" was stoned to death. He was so sure that a man killed on the cross could not be their Messiah. He became so incensed at the Christians that he decided he would do what he could to eradicate this heresy. Then Saul, "still breathing threats and murder against the disciples of the Lord, went to the high priest and asked him for letters to the synagogues at Damascus, so that if he found any belonging to the Way, men or women, he might bring them bound to Jerusalem" (Acts 9:1, 2).

The journey to Damascus, one hundred and fifty miles away, was a seven-day trip. As Saul and his men neared their destination, God broke through to Saul, the orthodox Jew. (He had to knock him down to wake him up.) A great light shone upon Saul, and he fell to the ground. Then he heard a voice, "Saul, Saul, why do you persecute me?" Saul cried, "Who are you, Lord?" The voice came back with the startling announcement, "I am Jesus, whom you are persecuting; but rise and enter the city, and you will be told what you are to do."

Saul found himself blinded by the experience and had to be led into the city. For three days he could not see and he could not eat—he had too much to think about. Then God sent Ananias to him. Now Ananias was one of the Christians at Damascus who had reason to fear Saul. He had heard how Saul had done evil to the Christians at Jerusalem and that he had come to Damascus to arrest all the Christians that he could find. The Lord appeared to Ananias in a vision and told him to go to the house of Judas on Straight Street and find the man from Tarsus, named Saul. Ananias had reason to hesitate, but the

Lord said, "Go, for he is a chosen instrument of mine to carry my name before the Gentiles and kings and sons of Israel; for I will show him how much he must suffer for the sake of my name." Ananias was convinced by the Lord and went to find Saul without any fear and met him with the assuring words, "Brother Saul, the Lord Jesus who appeared to you on the road by which you came, has sent me that you may regain your sight and be filled with the Holy Spirit." (Acts 9:1–22; 22:6–15; Gal. 1:11–19.) Saul received his sight, was filled with the Spirit, baptized, and took food. He was now ready for the ministry God had for him.

From this time Paul was turned out on the Greco-Roman world aflame with the Spirit and tireless in his preaching about Jesus as Messiah and Savior. He won converts everywhere and accepted them as Christians without any consideration for Jewish rites. He now knew salvation by grace and not by human effort through observance of old rites.

There were still rigid conservatives around who dogged Paul's steps. They confused his converts by seeking them out and telling them that no one could be saved unless he followed the laws of Moses. So Paul and Barnabas were sent to Jerusalem to have this matter settled. (Acts 15.) In the conference, after much debate, Peter told his experience with Cornelius, how God gave those Gentiles the Holy Spirit, making no distinction between the Gentiles and Jews, but that all were saved by grace. So the assembly kept silence—that is, the witness of the work of the Holy Spirit stopped all argument. And the question was settled—for the time being.

As Paul's work increased among the Gentiles, cultural problems were intensified. The Jewish Christians continued with dedication to the same God with a *new* understanding of God through Jesus Christ, but the Gentiles came from idolatrous background and their whole idea of God had to be changed. Besides *ideas* of God, drastic social changes had to be made. Great spiritual discernment was needed to know what these changes had to be to live in harmony with Christ and His way.

The contrasts between Christian culture and Jewish and pagan culture may be different from our contrasts today, but the method of discernment is the same. We, too, must learn the difference between a secular culture and what it really means to be Christian. Missionaries in other lands have learned much from the Apostle Paul. We know more about the church at Corinth than at any other place. When reading Paul's letter to the Christians at Corinth, we are startled to find the problems there so very like ours in the Western world.

But perhaps our most disturbing conflict in cultures is the one among those of us who have the most in common: Christians who say they love the Lord but do not love each other. Christians who condemn other Christians break our worldwide witness to our Lord more than anything else. By overemphasizing the things in which we differ, we lose relationship with God as well as with each other. What is wrong if denominations cherish their own heritage and their unique customs? Does it help to *fight* over interpretations and doctrines? Doctrines *are* important, interpretations *are* important, but when the most vehement "defenders of the faith" get on the warpath, God seems to be forgotten. It is a great surprise to some ardent Christians who demand much water baptism (that's my heritage!) to find another Christian filled with the Spirit of God who was only sprinkled, or even dry-cleaned like a Quaker! I have seen more emphasis at times on the amount of water than on the necessity to become new creatures in Christ. If only we could throw the real emphasis on the Lord Jesus Christ and His grace we would be slower to condemn others or their heritage. In fact, the only unity we can find is in Jesus Christ. We *don't make unity, we join it*.

We cannot organize for this unity; it comes only through the Spirit of God. We face the same issue all the early Christians faced: how much of my "faith" is from my cultural background and environment and how much is really from my relationship to the Lord Jesus Christ?

10 Reality in Religious Experience

Because he wrote so many letters to growing Christians we can learn more from the Apostle Paul than from anyone else about what it means to have a real experience of God. With his complete dedication to God through all of his personal life and the discipline of his theological training, Paul was able to think through what had really happened to him and to other Christians.

After the day of Pentecost those who had known Jesus in the flesh talked about the *Holy Spirit* as the source of their new power in life and service. Paul did not know Jesus as a man but met Him as the risen Lord, so he talked about being *in Christ*. Some scholars have said that Paul brought a different gospel from that which Jesus had proclaimed, or even from that which the first apostles preached, but the main difference came because Paul met Jesus as the *risen* Lord. We need never stumble over a change of vocabulary from Jesus to Peter to Paul.

A difference of vocabulary continues to bewilder people even to this day. Those of the "Holiness tradition" use a certain vocabulary, those of Pentecostal background use another. Lutherans, Presbyterians, Baptists, Catholics, all kinds of Brethren and Christians use whatever words they have at hand from their heritage, but when they get together to share in depth in the name of the Lord, somehow they *know* each other in the Spirit, regardless of their semantics, if they truly love the Lord.

Putting into words what an experience of God means is called theology. When a person begins with an experience of God it is one thing; but when he begins with theology *without an experience of God* it is quite another matter. The person who *experiences God* grows in godlikeness, but the person who knows only *about God* usually becomes hard and vindictive.

These vindictive ones make disruptive missionaries. It broke Paul's heart to learn what they did to new Christians: "I am astonished that you are so quickly deserting him who called you in the grace of Christ and turning to a different gospel—not that there is another gospel, but there are some who trouble you and want to pervert the gospel of Christ" (Gal. 1:6). The perversion of the gospel may be an overemphasis on part of a truth to the exclusion of the center of all real religious experience. God is the center as revealed in Christ, available to each one through the Holy Spirit.

This experience of the Spirit (Christ) is the norm for all those who give themselves in complete commitment to the Lord. This experience even comes to those who know no doctrine or theology of such a happening. The disciples are a witness to that. They had no idea what was going to happen on the day of Pentecost, but when that day came and the Promise was fulfilled, they knew with heart and mind: *This is it.* Paul is a particular help to us now because he, like us, came to his experience of Christ (the Holy Spirit) *after* the Ascension and *after* Pentecost day. He really belongs to our experience era, so whatever experience he had is also available to each one of us. Unfortunately, too many Christians are living as though Pentecost had never happened—even as though Jesus had never come. It is important to recognize and know our real heritage in Christ. Seeing Peter before Pentecost and the change in him afterward is a great challenge, but Paul leaves us with no excuse—he is of our time. Including his Jewish background, Paul could honestly say years later that he had lived his whole life "in all good conscience." (Acts 23:1; 24:16; 26:19.)

The very fact that Paul was so honest and faithful in following God created his greatest conscience problem concerning his Jewish days. He found it impossible to be faithful to all the laws and traditions which he had learned as a Pharisee. Pharisaic tradition elaborated three hundred and sixty-five prohibitions and two hundred and forty-eight commandments. There were one thousand five hundred and twenty-one Sabbath rules. And failure in one point made one guilty before the law the same as if he had failed in all points. No wonder Paul could cry out years later, "Wretched man that I am! Who will deliver me from this body of death?" (Rom. 7:24). He didn't know he was so miserable until after he found the way out through the grace of Jesus Christ.

The theme of joy and wonder runs through all Paul's writings —for the fact that the risen Lord would find him and come to him. James Stewart wrote of him in *A Man in Christ:*

That Jesus Christ, whose name he had maligned, whose followers he had harried, whose cause he had striven to bring down to destruction, should nevertheless have come to meet him, and to lay hands on him, was a thought at once gloriously uplifting and terribly subduing. . . . And never for a moment did he doubt the love that had come seeking him was the love of God himself. . . . All his feverish quest for peace and righteousness and certainty was now over, for God in Christ had taken the initiative. . . . The cataclysm of that hour ushered Paul into a totally different sphere of being. He was now as unlike the man who had set out from Jerusalem as noonday is unlike midnight, as life is unlike death. His outlook, his world, his moral sense of life-purpose— all were changed. He was a man in Christ.

Paul's own explanation of such an experience which began for him in that first encounter with the risen Lord is in his prayer for other Christians: "For this reason I bow my knees before the Father . . . that . . . he may grant you to be strengthened with might *through his Spirit in the inner man, and that Christ may dwell in your hearts through faith;* that you, being rooted and grounded in love, may have power to comprehend with all the saints what is the breadth and length and height and depth, and to know the love of Christ which surpasses knowledge, that you may be filled with all the fulness of God" (Eph. 3:14–19).*

The theme of Paul's whole witness concerned being "in Christ" or "Christ in me." He used such phrases as a fact of experience and not as theological statements. Whenever Paul spoke of the *indwelling Christ* or the *Spirit within*, he was always speaking of the same experience. The prayer for the Ephesians has *"Spirit in the inner man," "Christ dwelling in the heart,"* and *"Being filled with all the fulness of God."* These are not three different experiences but three different ways of expressing the same experience.

Some psychologists have referred to the *inner man* as the *unconscious* area of one's personality. In *Christian Life and the Unconscious* Dr. Ernest White, a Christian psychiatrist in London, designates the unconscious as the basic area of the Holy Spirit's work:

We perceive the world around us by means of our senses. God is not perceptible in the same way. We cannot directly perceive him by sight or hearing, or by touch. He is invisible except by faith. It is through the subliminal or unconscious area of our personalities that he does his work. The influence and the energy of the Spirit work in the depths. . . .

A new and supernatural driving-power has been introduced into the unconscious. A redirection of instincts and emotions takes place from the source. The Christian is not called upon to destroy or repress his instincts. He finds them redirected into new and useful channels of expression. Christ came that we might have life and have it more abundantly. . . . He came to liberate rather than suppress, thus bringing about a positive rather than a negative process. . . .

---

*Even though Paul's authorship of this letter is often questioned, many respected scholars do accept it. I like Markus Barth's comment that Paul did not need to be "Pauline," therefore the very argument used against his authorship is actually an argument for it.

When Christ dwells in the heart, a new motive, a new goal is given to all the forces latent in the mind, so that the whole direction of life and conduct undergoes alteration. Instincts are not crushed, they are given a new aim.

If the unconscious, our inmost soul, is the creative area of our being and the Holy Spirit is the creative Spirit of God whose main activity is in the unconscious, then this is the deepest kind of relationship possible to a human being—the Holy Spirit in the inner man, Christ in our hearts, and filled with the fullness of God. This is God-experience, indeed.

The work of the Holy Spirit deep in one's soul means that the basic work of the Holy Spirit is *quiet*. This is what Paul meant when he said, "If any one is in Christ, he is a new creation" (II Cor. 5:17). The new life and the new power were amazingly *natural* to the new Christians—it was a *new natural*. Jesus had said to His disciples, "I am with you, I will be *in* you." So the baptism of the Holy Spirit is the *personality* of Christ coming into one's innermost being to take up His abode there. Paul spoke of "Christ in me" in one way or another over one hundred and sixty times and he mentioned the Holy Spirit over a hundred times in what we have of his writings. This was his central theme.

The times that I have been guided and did not know it until later have amazed me more than the times when I knew beforehand what I felt sure was God's guidance. Jesus said the Holy Spirit would be our guide. We take His word for that as we keep up to date in our relationship with Him. He will never give me a vision at night to tell me where I need to grow if my husband already knows! He will simply tell me through Baxter. We must also do our homework. We do not need special visions for anything already clearly stated in His Word. In obedience we grow in our sensitivity to His will.

We have only our human vocabulary to express what the Lord has done for us, but even at that we are limited because an experience of God cannot be fully expressed or easily analyzed. Many scholars have tried to analyze just what happened to Paul on the Damascus road. They compare Luke's account in Acts with Paul's own accounts in his letters and seem bewildered—or critical. The secret is not in the details; it is in the fact of an encounter with the risen Lord and the dynamic change that came into Paul's life.

Even though Paul's initial experience of the risen Lord was so definite and startling, he never centered on his *experience* but witnessed always to the Christ who came to him. When he was criticized, Paul never defended himself, only his ministry which had been given to him by the Lord. There were times when Paul "boasted" of his own experiences, but these must be considered in context. (See II Corinthians, Chapters 11, 12.) The boasts were written ironically out of heartbreaking concern for new Christians led astray by self-seeking evangelists. It was the agonizing cry of a pastor's concern that made him cry out, "I think that I am not in the least inferior to these superlative apostles!"

One of the greatest dangers that follows the ecstasy or joy of an experience of the Lord is that one may feel he has "arrived" when actually he has only started in the most wonderful relationship possible to a human being. This dynamic assurance in the Lord can so easily be perverted from Christ-consciousness to a self-centered experience. Even *wanting* an experience like someone else's can be a perversion at the start. And an emphasis on one's own experience can lead "Jesus people," "Neopentecostals," or anyone who has a definite experience of God to expect others to have a like experience. It is so very important to keep the emphasis on the Lord Himself in order to have a real experience or to keep it real.

For himself Paul saw this clearly. He said, "I do not consider myself to have 'arrived,' spiritually, nor do I consider myself already perfect. But I keep going on, grasping ever more firmly that purpose for which Christ Jesus grasped me. My brothers,

I do not consider myself to have fully grasped it even now. But I do concentrate on this: I leave the past behind and with hands outstretched to whatever lies ahead I go straight for the goal—my reward the honor of my high calling by God in Christ Jesus. All of us who are spiritually adult should set ourselves this sort of ambition, and if at present you cannot see this, yet you will find that this is the attitude which God is leading you to adopt. It is important that we go forward in the light of such truth as we have ourselves attained to" (Phil. 3:12–16, Phillips).

To the Colossians Paul wrote a wonderful paean of praise to the Lord Jesus, then added, "And you, . . . he has now reconciled in his body of flesh by his death, in order to present you holy and blameless and irreproachable before him, *provided that you continue in the faith."* (Col. 1:15–23.) That "provided" is a challenge to growth, indeed. We can never rest on an *initial* experience of Christ (the Holy Spirit); we only start with it. "Babes in Christ" still need to grow.

Paul's phrase *"straining* forward to what lies ahead" (Phil. 3:13, RSV) is often misinterpreted. Paul was picturing an athletic race. He was not talking about the debilitating tension which incapacitates a person but about the strict, relentless discipline that sets an athlete *free.* The sportsman is not ready for a real race until he has trained enough to have this kind of freedom. Paul was not thinking of this kind of discipline *in order to attain* an experience of Christ. He meant the love discipline that *follows* an established relationship with Christ. As we go along day by day, God will always show us where we are still short of perfection, but we should hold to what we have already learned. In other words, if we are as far as high school we do not want to slip back to kindergarten in the school of Christian living.

Constant faith in the fact of the indwelling Christ makes possible the redeeming grace of the work of the Holy Spirit in one's life. There is real freedom from anxiety in such faith. We are free to grow. This process of growth is called sanctification:

"to be made holy." Sanctification means to be *set apart* and holy means *to be made whole.* Sanctification is the unfolding of the Christ character in the life of the one truly given to God. The changed character and disposition are fruit of the union with Christ. "But the fruit of the Spirit is love, joy, peace, patience, kindness, goodness, faithfulness, gentleness, self-control" (Gal. 5:22). Before Paul knew the Lord he had no love for those who disagreed with him, he had no patience or gentleness for "those who should know better," and he most likely justified himself in these harsh attitudes. He knew he had no goodness even though he lived in all good conscience. He had no joy or peace until he knew the way through the Holy Spirit. The self-control he mentions is from the Greek word for power, with the prefix "put in." There is no real self-control possible until there is God-control.

Paul told the Philippians to work out their own salvation because God was at work in their lives. (Phil. 2:12, 13.) Sounds confusing? Well, it is *always* hard to distinguish between God's part and our part in our lives and in all our relationships. Some try to do God's part and neglect their own responsibility in this relationship, others expect God to do everything. This latter attitude is as irresponsible as the one who is always saying, "Let George do it." To the Colossians Paul spelled out the process in man's responsibility in the new life in Christ. Paul knew that God never overrides the human will, that man always remains responsible for his choices. So Paul said, "*Seek* the things that are above," "*Set your minds* on things that are above." The "things that are above" are not any "pie in the sky" business, but very much the concern of everyday living. Then Paul supplies a list of things for us to vote against, most of which anyone would call sin. However, the last item on Paul's list catches most people of the Western world—"covetousness, which is idolatry." Our whole economy is set up to make us "covet"!

Then Paul made out a second list which goes deeper: "Anger, wrath, malice, slander, lying to one another, race consciousness." Another list tells us to make definite choices for other qualities: "Compassion, kindness, lowliness, meekness, patience, forgiveness and love." The qualities to "put on" are indeed the *fruit* of the Spirit, but still the choice remains with the Christian—to grow or not to grow. (Col. 3:1–25.)

The traits that are to be put to death are what psychologists and psychiatrists call the *seeming* or *pseudo self*. The things that are to be put on are of the real self. "The real self," said Karen Horney in *Neurosis and Human Growth*, "is the alive, unique, personal center of ourselves; the only part that can, and wants to grow. The pseudo self is the slave of his own 'pride system.'" Dr. Fritz Kunkel said, in *Creation Continues*, "Only a single-minded person can grow; all divided minds go astray, suffer and perish, at first inwardly and then outwardly. That is not a moral law, it is a simple and inexorable biological fact. If we do not use our margin of free choice, we shall be pushed by circumstances in the wrong direction. To avoid the conscious decision is an unconscious decision in favor of destruction. We had better take the risk, therefore, consciously and deliberately."

Actually the covetousness which Paul mentions is idolatry because it is putting *things* before God. The temptation to this kind of idolatry is very subtle, because the *thing* might be very good in itself. After the Israelites were free from captivity, they were no longer tempted to idols as such. In captivity the synagogue life and what Scripture they had became very important to them. After the return to their homeland they became known as the *people of the Book*.

Any person with chained imagination can become legalistically bound to the *words* instead of the *Word*. We cannot forget that it was *"men of the Book"* who crucified Jesus. Those churchmen of that day thought Jesus was unorthodox. In the name of Scriptural truth they killed Him. But Peter, filled with the Spirit, saw that they *meant* to be faithful: "I know that you acted in ignorance, as did also your rulers" (Acts 3:17). They had vested interests and so their spiritual insight was perverted.

Even in the name of Jesus Christ the same type of person tried to gain power in the early church. These people were called Judaizers who wanted to follow all the intricacies of the old law in addition to following Christ. They were the ones who got new Christians all mixed up and broke Paul's heart. Paul wrote to the young Christians, "Oh, my dear children, I feel the pangs of childbirth all over again till Christ be formed within you" (Gal. 4:19, Phillips).

When we want nothing but God's will, how can we be sure we are not falling into the same idolatry of legalism? Both sides are very clear in the life of Paul who lived in all good conscience throughout his life. But in the legalistic days he followed the law with desperation, he was hard on himself, and harder on all who did not agree with him. The followers of Jesus were "wrong," so he set out to dispose of them in the name of God and truth. As a Christian, the contrast was in his character first of all. He emphasized the love of God as he saw the need for gentleness, kindness, patience. He had been set free by the grace of God. His real experience of God through Christ had taken him from the *words* on a page to the real *Word* of the Living God.

It is a great day when we find out that we do not need to *defend* God and His Truth; we need only to *proclaim* it and live it.

11 When the Mirage Beckons

In his religious life the faithful Jew was zealously disciplined. For the Jewish Christian, freedom from anxious effort through the grace of God brought a real joy to be celebrated. But this celebration placed more emphasis on God and His greatness than on the worshiper's feeling and experience. It was a God-consciousness and not an experience-consciousness.

It was a different story when Christianity came to people out of a pagan background. The pattern of their religious lives was very self-centered. If there was discipline it was from fear or from their helplessness in times of need. They were taught that they had to placate their gods to receive any help, or they were to "cooperate" with the gods as in the fertility cults. This was true from the time of Baalism in Canaan to Paul's time in Greece where the temples featured sacred prostitution. After any such "religious experience" the people would go back to the affairs of daily living. Religious experience was, therefore, occasional and not actually a part of life.

The Christian churches in the Gentile world had problems never faced by the Jewish people who had worshiped the true God before. We have more information about the Corinthian church than about any other church. It is also astounding how much their problems sound like ours in the Western world today.

To understand what Paul wrote to the Corinthian church we need to understand Paul as well as the background of that church.

Paul was basically a counselor who understood and loved the people. When they were won to Christ, he carried the concern for them in his heart that a parent carries for a loved child. When Paul was away from them, he kept in touch by letters. He wrote to certain situations among the people with the hope that the Christians would not lose Christ as the center of their lives.

Perhaps no statement of Paul's has been more misused than *"I have become all things to all men."* I have heard this quoted many times as an excuse for compromising. But such an interpretation is a complete misreading of Paul's purpose or experience. Note what he really said in context: "For though I am free from all men, I have made myself a slave to all, *that I might win the more.* To the Jews I became a Jew, *in order to win Jews;* to those under the law I became as one under the law—though not being myself under the law—*that I might win those under the law.* . . . To the weak I became weak, *that I might win the weak.* I have become all things to all men, *that I might by all means save some.* I do it all *for the sake of the gospel,* that I may share in its blessings" (I Cor. 9:19–23).

Today we call this *"being involved."* Paul never did anything to gain a following for himself, only for his message and his Lord. He was uncompromising when it came to anything that might detract from the supremacy of the Lord Jesus Christ, but in peripheral matters, even though important to Paul, he could make adjustments in order to win people to Christ. Because Paul understood the background of his converts, he had mercy for them even when he scolded them. And we cannot understand what he wrote to them unless we also understand the nature and customs of these people to whom he wrote. Then we can also understand the particular problems they faced.

We must remember that Paul was thinking of *them* when he wrote. He was not thinking of us who would read his words so many centuries later. He did not realize he was writing "Scripture." But these letters written under the inspiration of the Holy Spirit are truly Scripture for us too because people are the same the ages through and the world around. That is the reason many of these letters sound as though Paul is writing to us in our day and about our very problems. People still have trouble getting along with each other; they still have marriage problems, they still have women's liberation problems, and they still have difficulty discerning authentic experiences of God. Just the same, Corinth is not New York or London or Chicago or Roanoke.

But we can find real help because Paul's correspondence with the Corinthians really probes the subtle intricacies of religious experience. The Gentiles in this city were extremely *religious* before they became Christian, and they were prone to fall back into old culture patterns because their consciences had not yet been fully trained. So we must know something about their old culture patterns to understand their "Christian" problems.

It was said that Corinth was made for greatness, but Julius Caesar did not dream that it would be remembered for the Apostle Paul more than for him! The city was on an isthmus between two good seaports. As a Greek city it was destroyed in 146 B.C. by the Romans and then rebuilt by Julius Caesar in 46 B.C. as a Roman colony which became the capital of Achaia. In Paul's day Corinth was a relatively new city with few traditions. It was a commercial city engrossed in making money. Its population was made up of Roman veterans, merchants, hucksters, Jews and Gentiles of all kinds, and thousands of slaves who were not even counted in the census. Corinth was famous for its pottery and its bronze. The unrivaled beauty of its bronze was created by women slaves who were forced to polish it with their bare arms until their skin was worn off. But Corinth's greatest fame was from the immorality sanctioned by its religion. It has been said that Greek immorality was at least aesthetic but that when the Romans adopted it they made it crude. To call a man or a woman a Corinthian anywhere in all of Greece or Italy of that day was to say that he or she was immoral or a drunkard.

There were temples in this city to eight pagan deities. Of most interest to us as background for Corinthian church problems are the temples to Asclepius and Aphrodite. Asclepius was the patron of medicine, the father of Hygeia. When this temple was excavated, all manner of organs and other parts of the human body made from terra cotta were found. Whenever anyone was healed he had an image made of the healed part of his body and brought it to the temple as a thank offering. The most famous temple in Corinth was the one to Aphrodite, the goddess of love. The Romans identified Aphrodite with Venus, the mother of Cupid. Her temple was the most conspicuous, situated on top of Acrocorinthus which rose above the city one thousand and fifty feet. A thousand priestesses were kept in this temple for the benefit of the worshipers! These girls were beautiful, carefully trained sacred prostitutes, and men came from everywhere to "worship." Then each evening the priestesses left the temple and came down on the streets of the city, attempting to seduce the men they met there. Gentlemen in Corinth didn't have to walk into temptation; it came to them! Out of this practice grew a Greek proverb: "Not every man can afford a journey to Corinth." In writing to the church in Corinth Paul lists all the kinds of people who cannot enter the kingdom of God, and adds, "and such were some of you." (I Cor. 6:9–11.)

One wonders how the Apostle Paul could ever have had the courage to preach the gospel in such a city and expect any results. But he started in the Jewish synagogue where he felt at home—for awhile—until he was put out, then he went next door to the home of Titius Justus, a God-fearing Gentile. There people became believers and were baptized. Jewish opposition continued to grow, but the Lord came to Paul one night in a vision and said, "Do not be afraid, but speak and do not be silent; for I am with you, and no man shall attack you to harm you; for I have many people in this city." Paul stayed there a year and six months, longer than he ever stayed in any other place. (Acts 18:1–11.) And so a church was established in this evil "inner city."

The membership list of the Corinthian church is most interesting: Titius Justus (Acts 18:7); Crispus, the former synagogue ruler (I Cor. 1:14); Erastus, the city treasurer (Rom. 16:23; Acts 19:22); Aquila and Priscilla, with whom Paul lived (Acts 18:2–3); Stephanas, the first convert (I Cor. 1:16; 16:15); Gaius (I Cor. 1:14; Rom. 16:23); Chloe (I Cor. 1:11); Phoebe (Rom. 16:1); the poor (I Cor. 1:26–28); slaves (I Cor. 7:22); dockyard workers; small tradesmen; free men; Jews and Gentiles. Every social class was there in one church fellowship from the slaves to top city officials.

No wonder there were problems in that social conglomeration! The first problem concerned cliques and factions. (I Cor. 1:10–17; 3:4–15.) But it's intriguing to note that these cliques were not according to cultural patterns but according to which preacher each clique idolized. Some said they belonged to the "Paul party," others to the "Apollos party," others to the "Peter party." Then others claimed to be the spiritual ones—they belonged to the "Christ party." Paul wanted them all to know that such quarreling did not become Christ's people, that Christ could not be divided.

Paul was concerned about this quarreling because it revealed to him that these rather new Christians did not yet know how to do God-thinking; they still thought in terms of worldly wisdom and did not perceive the wisdom that comes from God. So leadership or social background were not the determining factors but relationship to Christ through the Holy Spirit. Paul wrote: "Not many of you were wise according to worldly standards, not many were powerful, not many were of noble birth; but God chose what is foolish in the world to shame the wise, God chose what is weak in the world to shame the strong, God chose what is low and despised in the world, even things that are not, to bring to nothing things that are, so that no human being might boast in the presence of God. He is the source of your life in Christ Jesus, whom God made our wisdom, our righteousness and sanctification and redemption . . ." (I Cor. 1:26–30). Paul told them, further, that this wisdom can be understood only by the discernment that comes from the Holy Spirit: "The unspiritual man does not receive the gifts of the Spirit of God, for they are folly to him, and he is not able to understand them because they are spiritually discerned" (I Cor. 2:14). Paul wanted them to know that God never counted their background against them and with like discernment leadership status was no factor for prestige, that only the Spirit of God in one's life made one a real Christian.

Then Paul's understanding heart was still merciful toward them and he could plead: "But I, brethren, could not address you as spiritual men, but as men of the flesh, as *babes in Christ.* I fed you with milk, not solid food; for you were not ready for it; and even yet you are not ready, for you are still of the flesh. For while there is jealousy and strife among you, are you not of the flesh, and behaving like ordinary men? For when one says, 'I belong to Paul,' and another, 'I belong to Apollos,' are you not merely men? What then is Apollos? What is Paul? Servants through whom you believed, as the Lord assigned to each. I planted, Apollos watered, but *God gave the growth.*" (I Cor. 3:1–6.)

Immorality was also a big problem in the Corinthian church (Chapter 5). This, of course, is not surprising, considering the previous experience of many of the members before they were Christian as well as the mores of the community in which they lived. What is called the "new morality" today is what the Corinthians practiced before they were Christian. Paul taught them the "new morality" of that day. Because of the new freedom inherent in a Christian fellowship, those "babes in Christ" were not yet responsible in their freedom. They had in their midst a situation which was considered immoral even in wicked Corinth. The church members were considered responsible in this circumstance because they were indifferent to this evil. Paul told them they must use discipline so that the sinning one could be redeemed.

Being short on the new character possible through the Holy

Spirit, many members were still self-centered and therefore they had many grievances against each other. They were fighting "for their rights," but instead of settling their difficulties within the Christian fellowship, they were going to the pagan courts. Their publicized pettiness was no witness for a new life in Christ. Paul told them they should each be concerned for the other and that it was better to sacrifice their own rights for Christ's sake.

Such fighting in public is not uniquely a Corinthian matter. Not long ago I read about two women who had a hair-pulling fight in the very church in which they had been "saved" a short time before. The woman whose hair got pulled took the other woman to court. The judge asked, "What's the matter with you, starting a fight in a church?" One woman said, "We weren't in a church, we were in a church basement." The judge found the defendant guilty of assault, and in fining her twenty-five dollars he said, "I'm taking into consideration that you have been saved"! What witness is that for what it means to be "saved"?

God's love-discipline was new to the Corinthians, so it is not a surprise that they frequently fell back into old cultural and religious patterns. After all, they were surrounded in their city by religious prostitution. Many of the Christians must have been approached by those beautiful temple girls as they came into town in the evening. Many of them must have misinterpreted the new freedom they were supposed to have through the grace of God. Perhaps they thought it did not matter what the body did so long as the spirit was free. What did freedom really mean? And what did it really mean to be spiritual? These were questions they were mixed up on. Were these Christians the "spiritual" ones who helped to create divisiveness in the church?

The agnostic philosophy of that time considered the body to be the prison of the spirit. Paul had another idea. "Do you not know that your body is a *temple* of the Holy Spirit within you, which you have from God? You are not your own; you were bought with a price. So glorify God in your body." (I Cor. 6:-19-20.) This temptation is so subtle that Christians get caught to this day—"Anything is all right if you love." This seems to be the theme of our culture right now. The problem comes when "love" disappears. Perhaps it is time for Christians, as well as all people, to know God's definition of love.

The problems so far mentioned had been reported to Paul by Sister Chloe, but Paul also had a letter from the Corinthian church asking advice about other matters. They wanted to know how a real experience of Christ would relate to these matters. The first was in relation to marriage. They had many detailed questions ranging from such ascetic attitudes whereby husbands and wives should live together as brother and sister, avoiding all sex relations in order to be truly spiritual, to the other extreme of freedom or license for unfaithfulness to one's mate.

The astounding thing that Paul said to the Corinthians about husband and wife relationships is usually overlooked because too many people remember only that he advised them against marriage in the first place. (They forget that he expected the second coming of Christ very shortly. This was only circumstantial advice and no argument at all against marriage.) In Christ, Paul gave men and women the same status in their relation to each other: "For the wife does not rule over her own body, but the husband does; *likewise the husband does not rule over his own body, but the wife does*" (I Cor. 7:4). The first half of this statement was what they expected—and practiced—but the second half meant *revolution.* This was in line, however, with Paul's main thesis about men and women: that in Christ there is neither male nor female. (Gal. 3:28.)

Paul is so often misunderstood because people do not know the difference between the world's wisdom and God's wisdom. Paul said this revolutionary social change in marriage was possible *in Christ.* That means that neither one seeks selfish "rights"; each is concerned for the other and committed to the other. It means that Paul thought of each partner as a *person* and neither one as a "thing." Neither one can exploit the other for personal advantage, but each cherishes the other. The real insight that Paul had for human relations we shall see in the thirteenth chapter of his first letter to the Corinthians.

Another big question from the members of the church at Corinth had to do with idols. (I Cor. 10.) Every trip to the butcher shop involved a religious and ethical decision. Nearly all meat had previously been sacrificed to idols. For new Christians the thought of the meat having been used in worship could easily have been a pullback into old ways of worship. For Paul it meant nothing at all. He could eat it or not eat it. The fact that Paul had this freedom was very different from his days under the law. (See Lev. 11.) Now for Paul the whole issue was one of personal freedom in relation to others and to Christ and not a legalistic question. This Christian freedom seems paradoxical. Paul said, "For though I am free from all men, I have made myself a slave to all, that I might win the more" (I Cor. 9:19). This is chosen servanthood in Christ and has nothing to do with being exploited by another.

Actually, the issue is a matter of self-centeredness, which is the Biblical definition of sin. This selfishness turned up in every relationship. It even spoiled the fellowship at the Lord's supper. (I Cor. 10:14–22; 11:17–34.) Paul had to tell them that they were worse off spiritually for having gone to church! "When you meet together, it is not the Lord's supper that you eat. *For in eating, each one goes ahead with his own meal.*" One can be "religious" enough to go through the forms of worship and still miss relationship with Christ. "So that, whoever eats the bread or drinks the cup of the Lord with proper reverence" is making himself like one of those who allowed the Lord to be put to death without discerning who He was. "No, a man should thoroughly examine himself, and only then should he eat the bread or drink of the cup. He that eats and drinks carelessly is eating and drinking a judgment on himself, for he is blind to the presence of the Lord's body." (I Cor. 11:27–29, Phillips.)

In the sacred communion service Paul called for a thorough examination of one's spiritual condition. Is it merely religious form, or is it in truth an experience with God? It is always important to know whether or not a debated issue causing conflict is only cultural. A church membership cannot be divided on methods if they all love the Lord Jesus Christ. They cannot be divided on so-called loyalty to certain pastors or evangelists if their real allegiance is to the Lord. They cannot even be divided on their different religious experiences if they love Christ first of all.

We want the freedom the Apostle Paul found in his new life in Christ. We must face the fact that to be *in Christ* means that we choose servanthood as Christ did and as Paul did.

12 Mirage to Reality

With all their religiosity the strangest conflict in the Corinthian church was competitiveness in relation to their spiritual gifts. They forgot or didn't know the difference between the *Gift* of the Holy Spirit and the *gifts* of the Spirit. Immature self-centeredness was revealed again as they argued about which gift was the preeminent one. Paul did not want them to be uninformed about these spiritual gifts. (I Cor. Chapters 12, 14.)

Long ago F. B. Meyer said, "When we discuss *what* we believe we are divided but when we discuss *whom* we believe we come together." This is what Paul wanted the Corinthian church to see.

For Paul the *whom* was the most important fact. This is the place to begin any discussion of Christian experience and its authenticity. Through the Spirit, one can say *"Jesus is Lord."* (I Cor. 12:1–3.) As pagans the Gentiles had turned to idols "as they were taught," or, as another translator says, "as impulse directed." The old worship was a self-centered search for feeling, but for Paul the Christian experience meant the indwelling Christ—serving Him as Lord. In fact the early Christian "hello" was *"Jesus is Lord."* This is also what Jesus meant when He told the disciples about the coming of the Spirit, "He will glorify me, for he will take what is mine and declare it to you" (John 16:14). It is spontaneous to glory *in an experience of the Lord,* but it is subtly easy to fall into glorying in the experience itself. This is when a witness becomes arrogant and divisive and draws attention to himself instead of to the Lord.

Some people imply and others really say, "Unless you have an experience like mine, you do not have the real thing." Some who speak in tongues say this, and some who are *against* speaking in tongues also hold the same attitude. Both are emphasizing *self* instead of the Lord. Of course, I recognize that many who have just come into the new joy of an experience of the Lord sound as if they are emphasizing their feeling. But if the experience is really of the Lord, it will hold even when the early exuberance is tempered by daily difficulties. The important fact is that we should truly trust the Holy Spirit's work in other lives and not pass judgment on them. It is too easy to apply labels. And when we *push* people toward a certain experience, we retard them in their spiritual progress because we shift their attention from the Lord to a "feeling experience." The Holy Spirit can really be trusted to do His work.

There is one Lord, one gift of the Holy Spirit, but when it comes to the *gifts* of the Spirit there is a great variety. "To *one* is given through the Spirit the utterance of wisdom, and to *another* the utterance of knowledge according to the same Spirit, to *another* faith by the same Spirit, to *another* gifts of healing by the one Spirit, to *another* the working of miracles, to *another* prophecy, to *another* the ability to distinguish between spirits, to *another* various kinds of tongues, to *another* the interpretations of tongues. All these are inspired by one and the same Spirit, who apportions to each one individually as he wills." (I Cor. 12:8–11.)

This is true individuation, which means that each one can find abundant life without infringing on another's prerogative to fulfillment. This variety implies the potential of fulfillment for each of us. The Holy Spirit is the creative Spirit of God. I believe that no one can know his fullest personality development without God's Spirit. This means a far greater potential for fulfillment than can be expected from any vocational guidance test. We are considering not only innate possibilities but the plus that comes with God's Gift and the other gifts graciously bestowed as He knows best. One friend wrote, "God never gives me responsibilities my size: He always stretches me." It is when we are able to do more than could normally be expected of us that God really gets the glory. This variety in gifts also means that no person is a carbon copy of another.

When the variety of gifts is truly from God, all competitiveness is eliminated and each one is able to appreciate everyone else's gift. No gift from God is given just to guarantee a good feeling for the recipient; it is always given "for the common good" (I Cor. 12:7). This is the story from Abraham to Paul. God calls those who are responsive to Him so that they may be a blessing to the others whom He loves. A true manifestation of the Spirit in one's life gives freedom to minister to others, to understand them and to love them.

We need the fellowship of other people in the Lord, but *never* as a retreat from those who do not agree with us. It is a tendency for those of like faith to cluster together, but we meet in fellowship to be strengthened for service *outside* the fellowship. Jesus prayed, "As thou didst send me into the world, so I have sent them into the world" (John 17:18).

Of course, one enjoys the "fellowship of the saints," but even joy is a result and not a motivation. Paul likened this group fellowship in the Lord to the body which is one but has many members. Then follows the cartoon section of Paul's letter. (I Cor. 12:12–31.) Imagine the singer being mouth only! or the one who listens ears only! Every part of the body needs every other part, and if one member suffers, the whole body suffers. Anyone with a sore toe knows that. In the same way the church is a body —it is the body of Christ on earth. "And God has appointed in the church first apostles, second prophets, third teachers, then workers of miracles, then healers, helpers, administrators, speakers in various kinds of tongues. Are all apostles? Are all prophets? Are all teachers? Do all work miracles? Do all possess gifts of healing? Do all speak in tongues? Do all interpret?" The inference is that all do not do the same thing. But Paul said there is a more excellent way, the way of love which makes them one body. Being *part* of a body means that those with whom we live and work daily will get the first blessing out of any real experience of God we may have.

I sat next to George in a prayer group at a retreat. George was a sweet, strong man. He had been converted out of American paganism six years before and baptized in the Spirit four years later. He was lonely at home because his wife had not yet been converted. He asked prayer for her. I turned to him and said, "George, do you love her?" He was surprised, then he answered, "I try to." I said, "George, 'try to' is simply not enough for any woman. Love her as a husband as well as a Christian and she will want what you have." George thought for a moment, then said, "That explains what happened to me this morning. I thanked the Lord because He understood me and the Lord said to me, 'To whom can your wife go?'" That is exactly the point. The more we have of God's Spirit the more likely it is that others will know the God of love. "The Spirit is given for the common good."

I once taught a Bible study on the Corinthian church at a retreat. I did not know until later that one group was meeting daily to pray that I would say nothing against speaking in tongues and another group was meeting to pray that I would not say anything for the necessity of speaking in tongues. I answered the prayers of both groups because I stuck to the Apostle Paul! He made no brief *for or against* speaking in tongues, which the Corinthians emphasized more than any of the other gifts. Paul tried only to help them put their main emphasis on Christ and His love. He knew the dangers of seeking an experience rather than the Lord Himself. He wanted them to avoid the pattern of their former religious experience. We have a very dear friend, a missionary to India and America for the Assemblies of God. I have heard him say to Pentecostal groups, "If you seek tongues, you will never find the Lord; seek the Lord and take whatever He gives you." He knew what Paul was talking about: "Make love your aim," and since you are eager for manifestations of the Spirit, strive to excel in building up the church.

Paul himself rejoiced in the experience of speaking in tongues for his private praise and prayer. Some have suggested that this is what he meant in Romans 8:26: "Likewise the Spirit helps us in our weakness; for we do not know how to pray as we ought, but *the Spirit himself intercedes for us with sighs too deep for words.*" To the Corinthians he wrote, "I thank God that I speak in tongues more than you all; nevertheless, in church I would rather speak five words with my mind, in order to instruct others, than ten thousand words in a tongue" (I Cor. 14:19). The reason for this was: "He who speaks in a tongue edifies himself, but he who prophesies edifies the church" (I Cor. 14:4).

To Paul the issue was: Did they want religious experience as an end in itself, or did they want an experience of Christ through the Holy Spirit? This problem is as contemporary as today. Recently in a meeting I was handed a written question: "Do you go along with coaching people into voicing syllables to help them receive the gift of tongues?" This is the very issue to which Paul was speaking, the difference between a human striving to *"get" an experience* or a real gift from God when seeking Christ only. This question was old Corinth all over again.

Contrived tongues speaking was a familiar story to the Corinthians. Everyone knew about the oracles of Delphi. There was a place there where gases came out of a certain crevice in the rocks. In *The World of the Greeks* Victor Duruy describes how women seated on a tripod over the crevice "received the prophetic exhalations. Their faces paled, their limbs shook with convulsive movements. At first they uttered only whimpering complaints and groans; soon, with gleaming eyes and foaming mouth, their hair on end with fright, they were heard to speak, amidst cries of pain, broken incoherent words recorded with care and painstakingly put into verse by a priest, himself taken in by his faith in the oracle who had to discover the revelation of the future as hidden in these words by the god." This is the kind of manipulated experience which Paul warned against.

Paul touched the key to the difference between a Christ-experience of religious ecstasy and that of the pagan when he said, "Brethren, do not be children in your thinking; be babes in evil, but in thinking be mature" (I Cor. 14:20). Then he discussed the orderliness which should prevail in a Christian service which may include a hymn, a lesson, a revelation, a tongue, or an interpretation. But everything should be done for the *edification of all,* "For God is not a God of confusion but of peace" (I Cor. 14:33). By emphasizing the use of one's mind and maintaining the freedom of human choice, Paul was really saying that the closer to God one is even in ecstatic experience, the *freer the human will is.* This was never true in pagan religious ecstasy. It is not true in any *humanly contrived* experience today.

Faith healing was also familiar to the Corinthians. We know that faith itself has healing power up to a certain point. The temple to the god of healing was in the very center of their city. As Christians they must have known some healings that were beyond anything that ever happened in that temple to Asclepius. However, the Christians had fallen into competitiveness about the value of the different gifts. The advocates for healing thought they were better than those with other gifts. They had forgotten that God's gifts are for the use of God's love for all and never to provoke a competitive contest. Without love any gift has no real value and is spiritually pagan.

The concern today is not about the gift of healing in relation to other gifts, but in the limitation of healing. I know of a preacher who prayed for a very sick person and then he said to the patient, "Now I have faith that you will be healed. If you are not healed it is your fault for not having faith." This is cruelty —*not* the love of God. Then there are others who say that every accident and every tragedy is the will of God. One is arrogant and the other is fatalistic. Neither is Christian.

God created a world in which He limited Himself by giving

man the responsibility of choice. There is much evil in our
world. God overrides no man's will. Men of God are still killed
by evil men. The history of the Christian Church is full of martyrs. Even our Lord suffered a cruel death. In no case are we
God's pets; we are to be the priests and prophets of His redemp-
tive love. In any situation, no matter how serious or traumatic,
the greatest prayer is the same as our Lord's prayer, "Thy will
be done." This is not a lifeless, inactive prayer, it is not a self-
depressing prayer, it is a God-conscious prayer. After the list of
saints who suffered for God's sake in the eleventh chapter of
Hebrews we are told to look to Jesus "the pioneer and perfecter
of our faith, who *for the joy that was set before him endured the
cross"* (Heb. 12:2). The cross was not the end for our Lord, it was
only "on the way" as He followed the Father's will. If suffering
comes to me I must pray, "Lord, if by this suffering Thy name
can be hallowed, I accept it to be used for Thy glory." The cross
of Jesus is our Christian symbol. But His cross was not jewelry,
neither was it gold or shining brass.

Of course God wants His children to be well. He also wants
to reach everyone in the world with His love. We dare not think
we are God's special pets. During the recent floods in our city
I stood at the end of our front walk and watched the torrents
of water come down the street toward our house. Of course, I
prayed. When the waters stopped at the mail box and began to
recede, I thanked God, but I could not say I had been specially
favored by God. Too many saints were inundated! I have had
instant divine healing (when far from a doctor in India). I have
also been healed by a doctor's skill. In each case prayer cleared
the way for God's healing. But my beloved brother died of
cancer. I do not ask why. May God be praised even in and
through suffering is the real prayer.

It was not only freedom from suffering, but freedom itself
that the Corinthians were concerned about. I must admit that
the women were a definite part of the confusion in the church.
The women who became Christian had a new freedom which

they had never known before. Paul must have told them, too, that in Christ there is neither male nor female. Their men must have permitted this new freedom. But they did not yet know how to use it. Paul had to chide them: "What! Did the word of God originate with you, or are you the only ones it has reached?" (I Cor. 14:33–36.) We know that this was not Paul's attitude toward all women in the church from his mention of other women who were co-workers with him and helpful as church leaders. The Corinthians knew Priscilla as Paul's fellow worker in Corinth and Phoebe who was a deaconess in the church nearby. They must have heard of many others whom he honored. (Rom. 16:1–16; Phil. 4:2, 3.) Paul also was guest in the home of Philip, the father of four daughters who were preachers. (Acts 21:8, 9.) So the point Paul made in Corinth was only against the women who did not know how to use their new freedom.

The most relevant test that Paul gave for identifying an authentic experience of God was love. This is the heart of the matter, for *God is love.* "Love is of God, and he who loves is born of God and knows God. He who does not love does not know God" (I John 4:7, 8). Jesus said, "By this all men will know that you are my disciples, if you have love for one another" (John 13:35). Lack of love is the greatest heresy. Paul said to the Corinthians, "If I speak in the tongues of men and of angels, but have not love, I am a noisy gong or a clanging cymbal. And if I have prophetic powers, and understand all mysteries and all knowledge, and if I have all faith, so as to remove mountains, but have not love, I am nothing. If I give away all I have, and if I deliver my body to be burned, but have not love, I gain nothing" (I Cor. 13:1–3). Imagine how this sounded to the Corinthians when it was read to them in their church meeting.

Paul avoided being argumentative about rating the different gifts of the Spirit. The people had already argued too much about them. He wanted them to see "the more excellent way," the God-way of love. In translation we often miss the meaning of what Paul really said about love and then we do not hear what the Corinthians heard. The word for love was formerly translated "charity," but the English word "charity" has lost its original meaning. Now the word "love" is too often thought of as Aphrodite would have used it. To avoid such misinterpretations many people have appropriated in English the Greek word *agape*. There were four Greek words for love, but *agape* was seldom used by the Greeks. It was left clean for Christian usage.

Agape demands the exercise of the whole man. William Barclay, in *More New Testament Words*, comments: "It has to do with the mind: it is not simply an emotion which rises unbidden in our hearts; it is a principle by which we deliberately live. . . . *Agape* is the spirit which says: 'No matter what man does to me, I will never seek to do harm to him; I will never set out for revenge; I will always seek nothing but his highest good.' " Such a love is bound to be the product of the Spirit. Such love is a gift of the Spirit and is not possible except through God's Spirit.

If we keep this Greek meaning in mind, we can better understand what the Corinthian church heard when Paul's letter was read to them. If the Corinthians really examined themselves, they must have wondered if they had any experience of God at all.

With this definition of love we can take our own examination of our spiritual status by substituting *I* for *love* in I Corinthians 13:4–7:

> I am patient and kind;
> I am not jealous or boastful;
> I am not arrogant or rude.
> I do not insist on my own way;
> I am not irritable or resentful;
> I do not rejoice at wrong.
> I bear all things,
> I believe all things,

I hope all things,
I endure all things.

"So faith, hope, love abide, these three; but the greatest of these is love" (I Cor. 13:13). Love is the *movement* of the Holy Spirit and the first characteristic of the Presence of the Holy Spirit in one's life.

Lest we feel too guilty in this examination, we must remember that this is God's love and we need never endure guilt. We look to Him in all honesty and His love clears the record and today becomes a new day. We remember what Paul said to the Galatians about love being the first fruit of the Spirit. He added, "If we live by the Spirit, let us also *walk* by the Spirit." (Gal. 5:22, 25). We *walk* step by step, which means we grow spiritually continuously. The *growing power* is the Holy Spirit power within. Anything that happens can be used toward the maturing process. (Eph. 4:13.)

The fact that God is the major factor in real spiritual experience is well stated by Hannah Whitehall Smith in her book, *My Spiritual Autobiography*. After telling of the time the Holy Spirit took over in her life, she said:

Suddenly something happened to me. What it was or how it came I had no idea, but somehow an inner eye seemed to be opened in my soul, and I seemed to see that after all God was a fact—the bottom fact of all facts and that the only thing left to do was to find out all about him. It was not a pious feeling, such as I had been looking for, but it was a conviction. . . . I did not discover everything at once. Like all novices, I grasped many half truths, and came to many false conclusions. But the search of itself was delicious, and the finding out of one's mistakes far surpassed the mortification of having made them. My soul had started on its journey of discovery—I needed no longer to work for my soul's salvation but only to work out the salvation that had been bestowed upon me. . . . It was no longer "How do I feel" but always "What does he say."

The gift of *love* means a new natural love for God, a terrific hunger for His Word, a new joy in prayer, a new love for others that brings endless surprises in human relationships. Another surprise is an unimaginable *peace*, so dynamic that one wonders how anything so quiet could be so powerful. This peace is part of the Promise, "Peace I leave with you; my peace I give to you" (John 14:27). Too often we forget that Jesus talked about this peace when He knew he would be murdered the next day! This is powerful peace.

Among all Spirit-filled people joy is one of the most outstanding words. This is a different kind of joy from what the world talks about. Like love and peace it is not primarily a feeling. It is much deeper than that. In times of difficulty and sorrow, joy becomes sheer gratitude for an understanding heavenly Father. Even the most devout in the kingdom of His love can miss the exuberance of joy when they suffer in times of illness. Dr. Nels F. S. Ferré was one of the Christian world's most respected theologians, but the greatest thing about him was the amazing simplicity of his faith and his relationship to the Lord Jesus Christ. I spent a day with him and his wife in October following his severe January heart attack. Brother Nels told me that he had not been able to sleep much for months before the heart attack but that he didn't mind because he would lie in bed all night rejoicing in fellowship with the Lord. After the attack the doctor made him take sleeping pills. Like a child he said to me, "I miss my nights of joy." I answered him according to truth which I had really learned from him! "Why, Brother Nels, you don't need joy, you have the Lord!" His face brightened as he exclaimed, "That's right!" Later he was talking about going back to his teaching the following Friday. He said, "But I don't have the power I had before!" I had to say, "But Brother Nels, you don't need the power until next Friday at eleven o'clock." With great relief he said, "That's right!" The next Friday I was at home in Virginia and at nine in the morning I dialed the Ferrés' Ohio number. Brother Nels answered. I said, "Brother Nels, I just want to remind you that the power of God will be

poured out at eleven o'clock this morning and to say God bless
you." The following week I received a letter from him, which
read like the book of Acts. It *was* the acts of the Holy Spirit.
When he died a few months later, I wrote to his wife, "Isn't it
wonderful that he died in his sleep? Now the pills can't do
anything to his joy!"

Patience, kindness, goodness, gentleness, were not natural
qualities for the Apostle Paul, but they became natural to the
"new man in Christ." In his old life faithfulness and self-control
demanded an agonizing discipline, but now both were a joy as
he trusted the indwelling Christ. That is what the grace of God
means.

For Paul the grace of God was very definitely related to the
resurrection of Christ, so he was glad when the church asked
about the resurrection. He loved to talk about the risen Lord:
"Now I would remind you, brethren, in what terms I preached
to you the gospel, which you received, in which you stand, by
which you are saved, *if you hold it fast—unless* you believed
in vain. For I delivered to you as of *first importance* what I also
received, that Christ died for our sins . . . , that he was buried,
that he was raised on the third day" (I Cor. 15:1-4). Then Paul
listed the post-resurrection appearances. All these appearances
were made to the disciples before the ascension *except* the
appearance to Paul, which came after the ascension. From his
own encounter the Apostle Paul learned to know Jesus as a
living Lord, a contemporary Presence, seen or unseen, the indwelling Christ, the fullness of the Holy Spirit. This puts Paul's
experience of the risen Lord in our era with the assurance that
whatever was available to him is also available to us.

Even though Paul counted himself unworthy he could, with
his whole heart, say, "But it is through the love of God that I
am what I am, and the *love that he showed me has not been
wasted*" (I Cor. 15:10, 20th Century Translation). Paul is one
person who never wasted the love of God but let it flow through
him to all the people whom he loved for Christ's sake.

The first priority in Christian experience is the love of Christ made possible through the Holy Spirit. We each carry the responsibility for others to know the love of God. May I quote my granddaughter, Kathy, who is an airline stewardess? She has not always seen love in church people. I'm sure she has wondered at times about God Himself. Not long ago, I was delighted when Genie Price asked me to bring Kathy along when I went to visit her and Joyce Blackburn. Genie, Joyce, and I had our usual joy and laughs in the Lord together, and as naturally as you please Kathy entered into our fellowship! Afterward she wrote to Genie, "You people were what God is all about and it hit home more than anything else ever has." You see why I am glad to dedicate this book on Christian experience to Genie.

For a summary of real experience of God, Paul said it so much better than I can: "For the love of Christ controls us, because we are convinced that one has died for all; therefore all have died. And he died for all, that those who live might live no longer for themselves but for him who for their sake died and was raised. From now on, therefore, we regard no one from a human point of view. . . . Therefore, if any one is in Christ, he is a new creation; the old has passed away, behold, the new has come. All this is from God, who through Christ reconciled us to himself and gave us the ministry of reconciliation; that is, God was in Christ reconciling the world to himself, not counting their trespasses against them, and entrusting to us the message of reconciliation. *So we are ambassadors for Christ, God making his appeal through us.*" (II Cor. 5:14–21.)

13 Reality in Witnessing and Service

Chosen to be ambassadors! Everything an ambassador does in a foreign country reflects on the country he represents; he is never only an individual. "We are ambassadors *for Christ, God making his appeal through us*"! We must remember that when we witness for Him it must be *God's appeal* more than "my experience" appeal. The *self*-conscious witness who says or implies, "You must have an experience like mine," is arrogant; the *God-conscious* witness is always humble and appealing. This is the reason Jesus said the Holy Spirit would glorify Him. A witness made through the power of the Holy Spirit is God making His appeal through us.

We are made new creations in Christ for this very purpose, for God to reach through to others. Robert Coleman in *Dry Bones Can Live* warns against a possible retardation in our Christian lives: "Many of us spend so much energy cultivating our piety that we make it a substitute for active evangelism. We get so wrapped up in our worship exercises, deeper life conventions, and sometimes even our meetings for revival, that we have no time or energy for real soul-winning. Certainly we must feed our souls by Bible study and spiritual meditation, but spiritual indigestion will likely occur if this devotion does not find an outlet in practical service."

The blessing never stops with us. Abraham was called to be a blessing to all nations. From Abraham to Paul it was a *call*, a *covenant* of relationship, which is our reconciliation with God, and then always followed by a *commission:* "Entrusting to us the message of reconciliation." It is astounding that God trusts us with the message of reconciliation, but that trust is contingent upon the power of the Spirit. When Jesus faced death, from a human standpoint His life was a failure, but He had full faith in the coming Holy Spirit.

When Jesus prayed for His disciples on the night before His death, He said, "As thou didst send me into the world, so I have sent them into the world." If we are being sent into the world, we can never remain huddled together in a fellowship caucus. We meet to be strengthened for going into the world. We need spiritual strength for those contacts. Jesus had prayed, "I do not pray that thou shouldst take them out of the world, but that thou shouldst keep them from the evil one." We are to be *in the world but not of it.* We are ambassadors.

The hardest thing for Christians to learn is how to be against the evil in the world and still love the people of the world. Paul recognized this when he said, "God was in Christ reconciling the world to himself, not counting their trespasses against them." We, as church people, have been very prone to be against the people in the world rather than the evil in the world. We have accused the people of their sins and they feel attacked and unloved. They want to avoid the church and church people and then they miss the good news of reconciliation. This is the reason the "unchurched" do not come to church. They need love not accusation. Only through the Holy Spirit-instilled love of God can we understand how God does not count their sins against them. Karl Barth once said that God does not count our sins against us, only our unwillingness to have them forgiven. When we "attack" people they become defensive and close the door to God's appeal. We must open that door, or make it easy for them to do so.

In social issues today church members have been prone to be against those who take opposite sides on an issue. In a certain board meeting we were having a lively discussion on the lettuce boycott. One person of Quaker background said we had a responsibility to growers as well as to laborers, that the church's ministry and responsibility was in reconciliation. An active protester in the group retorted, "You make me tired, you are always sitting on the fence." For the first time I saw that there was a real difference between reconciliation and "sitting on the fence." The one who "sits on the fence" is one who cannot take a stand on an *issue,* but reconciliation is about *people,* understanding the *need of the people on each side* of an issue. According to the teaching of Jesus, this is true even to the point of loving one's enemies.

The social activists of today are very good at protesting against corruption, but some also attack the people with whom they differ. Even though they may have honest compassion for the exploited and dispossessed, they show it in such a way that they make it impossible to witness to the oppressor. John Woolman, a great Quaker, did better. He fought ardently against slavery in the eighteenth century but tried to win as friends the very people he protested against. Even Mahatma Gandhi had this same ability to distinguish between issues and people. He said in *All Men Are Brothers,* "It is the acid test of non-violence that in a non-violent conflict there is no rancour left behind, and in the end the enemies are converted into friends. This was my experience in South Africa with General Smuts. He started with being my bitterest opponent and critic. Today he is my warmest friend."

Because of the violence of war and oppression "non-violence" has been very popular in recent years, but without love it is violent. Jacques Ellul, a social critic and French lay theologian, said in *Violence* that even though they cannot counsel the poor and oppressed to be submissive and accepting, "radicalism forbids participation in violence of any kind . . . it will serve as mediator between the powerful and the oppressed."

Of course, we must admit that every man cannot be won as

a friend, even when approached with love. Jesus was crucified, but no matter what evil His enemies did to Him, they got nothing but love out of Him because He was love. He prayed for His tormentors, and we know now that "God was in Christ reconciling the world to Himself, not counting their trespasses against them." Also we must remember that the cross was not the end of the redemption story. God's will was the only goal of Christ's life, and the cross was on that way of obedience. When we face difficulties and persecutions, we are reminded to be "looking to Jesus the pioneer and perfecter of our faith, who *for the joy that was set before him* endured the cross, despising the shame, and is seated at the right hand of the throne of God" (Heb. 12:2).

It happens that I have a collection of crosses given me by many friends. Each cross is beautiful. The crosses in our churches are all beautiful. They are conducive to singing about joy and victory. The cross of Jesus was ugly and cruel. A friend of ours, when in Palestine, made a special study of the Roman cross. When he returned he described the cross of Jesus to his congregation. A carpenter in the church said he would make one. It was to be used in the Good Friday service. The carpenter brought it to the church early Friday morning and said he must carry it himself up the steep steps in the front of the church. He stumbled and fell under the weight of the cross, which doubled its meaning for him. Then the cross was set up before the beautiful altar in the church. The chairman of the worship committee was watching, and as the cross was put in position she exclaimed, "What shall we do? It doesn't fit." That's our problem—relating the cross of Christ to the joy we find in His life and service. The joy in doing the Father's will is a different kind of joy from what the world means by joy. Many new Christians so full of the "joy of the Lord" are not prepared always for this deeper *joy*.

Some emphasize the joy and some emphasize the cross, and at times we misunderstand one another. This whole issue became much clearer to me when I received a very brotherly letter from a "radical theologian" whom I honor very much and disagree with on some issues. He wrote, "I know you have not been completely happy with the protesters and with me from time to time. I have regarded some of our differences as resulting from the proclamation of different accents of the gospel. I have stressed more a theology of the cross, the teaching that faithfulness to the gospel often brings a sword, conflict, especially with powers and principalities. Deep compassion for those who are being killed calls me for radical witness which does not always mean successful reconciliation but rather a cross. You have accented the gospel truths pointing to the joy and fruits one can know of living in Christ Jesus."

This brother's letter cleared for me the fact that reconciliation and the cross are not incongruous, but that the cross is an integral part of the reconciliation process. Then I also remembered a new Christian who was "persecuted" for her experience of the Lord, and she was feeling very sorry for herself and justified herself against her critics. She had forgotten entirely her responsibility for reconciliation, if she had ever known it. I told her the martyrs never knew they were persecuted. The ever-present danger is that any experience, joyous or difficult, can be turned into a *self*-experience when it should make one even more Christ-conscious. If the Christ-consciousness goes, the love leaks out also. When love goes, one can still be extremely religious, but he will get people and issues all mixed up and will be hard on all those who do not agree with him.

In any time of special evangelistic emphasis the old issue of evangelism *vs.* social service becomes rife. The truth is that it is never one *or* the other. Real Christian service is an outgrowth of a real experience of God; it is the call, the covenant relationship *plus* the commission. Social service as a mere end in itself is usually very unacceptable to the ones served. They seem to sense the self-consciousness in it. In the race riots several years ago a certain group of Christians who seemingly sacrificed everything for the blacks were the first ones attacked in the riots. Did the blacks feel "stooped down to"? To be called a "do-gooder" these days is to be discredited. It is the self-conscious-ness of it that is the curse.

The text used more than any other for social service is the last judgment scene in the parable Jesus told. (Matt. 25:31–46.) "As you did it to one of the least of these my brethren, you did it to me." The ones who were accepted said, "Lord, *when* did we see thee hungry and feed thee . . . ?" They were unconscious of having done any special religious service. The ones who were rejected asked, "When did we not do you service?" Evidently they thought they had done it. They most probably kept a record of their good deeds! Religious service is real when it is the spontaneous outgrowth of the love of Christ in any person's heart.

Religious witness is real when it is a *sharing* of good news because others are loved. David Augsburger said it well: *"Wit-ness is Withness:* More Showing than Telling." Jesus was reality in witnessing. Two good illustrations are in the stories of the Samaritan woman in the fourth chapter of John and the blind man in the ninth chapter. Jesus did not come *at* the people with *His* experience. He came to the people with love, met them where they were, and made them curious and hungry. He al-ways had them coming toward Him, and when they were ready, He told them His good news. Abraham Vereide, the founder of the International Christian Leadership movement (President's breakfast, etc.), discovered this secret. It was said of him that "he fanned the faintest spark of faith in a man rather than quenching it." This was the method of Jesus. He met *peo-ple*—with love and not argument. *He was His message.*

Witnessing is so much more than words. Some feel that they must buttonhole so many a day "to make their witness." People then feel grabbed and pushed around. Those who depend on words as witness are really stranded when words have no value —at least for a time. Wives with non-Christian husbands were told that their husbands should be won "without a word by the *behavior* of their wives" (I Pet. 3:1).

People seem to know when "evangelism" is words only. They recognize it as propaganda and steel themselves against it. Some years ago a certain church in Illinois reported its goal for new adherents. The day the article was in the paper I was seated in front of two men on a street car. They were discussing this church report. One man said, "They won't get me as one of their new statistics." Elton Trueblood, who saw the artificiality of such witnessing, wrote in *The Company of the Committed:* "The widespread aversion to evangelism seems to rest largely on our difficulty in distinguishing between it and proselytizing. Evangelism is the effort to facilitate the growth of new life, while proselytizing is the effort to enhance the power, prestige, or numbers of one's own particular sect or organization." People sense the difference between the real evangelist and the proselytizer. Something subtle happens to the evangelist who becomes tainted with proselytism; he forgets that results are for God's record, not his.

When caught by age or physical disability, even the best of evangelists and pastors can be taken off guard and trapped into an aching loneliness and a feeling of loss at not being needed, but they can find a real ministry in just *being* representatives of the Lord.

I have just had a day with a couple, retired after over fifty years of "successful" ministry. I expected a streak of dark regret for the home they gave up and the kind of ministry that was now in the past. But they have no regrets because they rejoice in the Lord daily and in that rejoicing witness to all their new friends. People are still people to them. They are merely transplanted in the kingdom of God to a quieter area, spreading the "fragrance of the knowledge of [Christ] everywhere" (II Cor. 2:14).

A real experience of God is never blotted out by anything that can happen to us. The Apostle Paul witnessed to this: "This

priceless treasure we hold, so to speak, in a common earthen-
ware jar—to show that the splendid power of it belongs to God
and not to us. We are handicapped on all sides, but we are never
frustrated; we are puzzled, but never in despair. We are persecuted, but we never have to stand it alone: we may be
knocked down but we are never knocked out!" (II Cor. 4:7–9,
Phillips).

We have learned from God's Word that *God is,* that He
reaches out to us before we even realize it, that He hopes for
and plans relationships with us, and that He wants us to be His
representatives on this earth. "So we are ambassadors for
Christ, God making his appeal through us." Our responsibility
is to respond to Him, and we may then know the fullness of His
love, which is authentic religious experience. A friend of mine,
Ernestine Hoff Emrick, said this:

> There was a time when God seemed far away,
> So high above this spot where I hold sway.
> And how I prayed that He would come and be
> A living Presence, very near to me,
> But now I know what cannot be forgot,
> He was here all the time—but I was not.

THE MIRAGE

If I speak in the tongues of men and of angels, but have not love, I am a noisy gong or a clanging cymbal.

And if I have prophetic powers, and understand all mysteries and all knowledge, and if I have all faith, so as to remove mountains, but have not love, I am nothing.

If I give away all I have, and if I deliver my body to be burned, but have not love, I gain nothing.

I Corinthians 13:1–3

THE REALITY

Love is of God, and he who loves is born of God and knows God. . . . God is love.

I John 4:7, 8

By this all men will know that you are my disciples, if you have love for one another.

John 13:35

Suggestions for Further Reading

There is great variety in the opinions and interpretations of authors. Even the ones I do not agree with help me to think more clearly. Every sincere, honest writer has something to contribute.

Background Books for Study

BEWER, JULIUS A. *The Prophets.* Harper & Row, 1949, 1955.

BRUCE, F. F. *New Testament History.* Anchor-Doubleday, 1972.

BROWNRIGG, RONALD. *Who's Who in the New Testament.* Holt, Rinehart and Winston, 1971.

CONWAY, JOAN. *Who's Who in the Old Testament.* Holt, Rinehart and Winston, 1971.

DEVAMBEZ, PIERRE, and others. *The Praeger Encyclopedia of Ancient Greek Civilization.* Praeger, 1966.

DURUY, VICTOR. *The World of the Greeks.* Minerva S.A. Geneve, 1971.

ELMSLIE, W. A. L. *How Came Our Faith?* Scribner, 1949.

FRANK, HARRY T. *Bible, Archaelogy, and Faith.* Abingdon, 1971.

FROMM, ERICH. *You Shall Be As Gods.* Fawcett, 1966. Even though Fromm does not believe in a personal God, every Christian should read what he says about idolatry and about the prophets.

GAER, JOSEPH. *The Lore of the Old Testament.* Little, Brown & Co., 1952.

KERENYI, C. *The Religion of the Greeks and the Romans.* Dutton, 1962.

PARMELEE, ALICE. *A Guidebook to the Bible.* Harper Chapel Book, 1948.

PFEIFFER, CHARLES F., and VOS, HOWARD F. *The Wycliffe Historical Geography of Bible Lands.* Moody Press, 1967.

PHILLIPS, J. B. *New Testament Christianity.* Macmillan, 1956.

Books About Jesus

BARCLAY, WILLIAM. *Jesus As They Saw Him*. Harper & Row, 1962.
————. *The Mind of Jesus*. Harper & Row, 1960, 1961.
BOWIE, WALTER RUSSELL. *The Master: A Life of Jesus Christ*. Scribner, 1958.
BUTTRICK, GEORGE A. *Christ and History*. Abingdon, 1963.
FILSON, FLOYD V. *Jesus Christ: The Risen Lord*. Abingdon, 1941.
MARNEY, CARLYLE. *He Became Like Us*. Abingdon, 1964.
MORRISON, MARY C. *Jesus: Man and Master*. World Publishing Co., 1968.
NEIL, WILLIAM. *The Life and Teaching of Jesus*. Lippincott, 1965.
PHILLIPS, J. B. *When God Was Man*. Abingdon, 1955.
ROWLINGSON, DONALD T. *Jesus the Religious Ultimate*. Macmillan, 1961.
SMART, JAMES D. *The Quiet Revolution*. Westminster, 1969.
TAYLOR, VINCENT. *The Life and Ministry of Jesus*. Abingdon, 1955.
THIELICKE, HELMUT. *Christ and the Meaning of Life*. Harper & Row, 1962.

Books About Paul

BAIRD, WILLIAM. *Paul's Message and Mission*. Abingdon, 1960.
BARCLAY, WILLIAM. *The Mind of St. Paul*. Harper & Row, 1958.
BARTH, MARKUS. *The Broken Wall*. Judson, 1959.
BORNKAMM, GUNTHER. *Paul*. Harper & Row, 1971.
DEISSMANN, ADOLF. *Paul: A Study in Social and Religious History*. Harper & Row, 1912, Torchbook, 1957.
HUNTER, ARCHIBALD M. *The Gospel According to St. Paul*. Westminster, 1966.
KINSEY, ROBERT S. *With Paul in Greece*. Parthenon, 1957.
KNOX, JOHN. *Chapters in a Life of Paul*. Abingdon, 1950.
KRAELING, EMIL G. *I Have Kept the Faith*. Rand McNally, 1965.
MACKAY, JOHN A. *God's Order*. Macmillan, 1953.
MUGGERIDGE, MALCOLM, and VIDLER, ALEC. *Paul: Envoy Extraordinary*. Harper & Row, 1972. Based on BBC TV film.
SHRADER, WESLEY. *Forty Days Till Dawn* (imagined memoirs of Paul). Word, 1972.
STEWART, JAMES S. *A Man in Christ*. Harper & Row, 1935.

TRESMONTANT, CLAUDE. *St. Paul and the Mystery of Christ.* Harper & Row, 1958.

Books on the Holy Spirit

BARCLAY, WILLIAM. *Flesh and Spirit.* Abingdon, 1962.
LEHMAN, CHESTER K. *The Holy Spirit and the Holy Life.* Herald Press, 1959.
NICHOL, JOHN THOMAS. *Pentecostalism.* Harper & Row, 1966.
SHERRILL, JOHN L. *They Speak with Other T ngues.* Spire Books, 1964.
STAGG, FRANK; HINSON, GLENN; and OATES, WAYNE E. *Glossolalia.* Abingdon, 1967.
VAN DUSEN, HENRY P. *Spirit, Son and Father.* Scribner, 1958.
WALKER, ALAN. *Breakthrough: Rediscovery of the Holy Spirit.* Abingdon, 1969.

Books on Prayer

BARCLAY, WILLIAM. *The Plain Man Looks at the Lord's Prayer.* Fontana, 1964.
BELDEN, ALBERT D. *The Practice of Prayer.* Harper & Row, 1954.
BUTTRICK, GEORGE A. *Prayer.* Abingdon, 1942.
CASTEEL, JOHN L. *Rediscovering Prayer.* Association Press, 1955.
DAY, ALBERT E. *An Autobiography of Prayer.* Harper & Row, 1952.
HARKNESS, GEORGIA. *Prayer and the Common Life.* Abingdon, 1948.
READ, DAVID H. C. *Holy Common Sense.* Abingdon, 1966.
STEERE, DOUGLAS V. *Dimensions of Prayer.* Harper & Row, 1962.

Books on the Church

ARNOLD, EBERHARD. *Salt and Light.* Plough Publishing House, 1967.
ARNOLD, EMMY. *Torches Together.* Plough Publishing House, 1964.
BRIGHT, JOHN. *The Kingdom of God.* Abingdon, 1953.
COLEMAN, ROBERT E. *Dry Bones Can Live Again.* Revell, 1969.
CULLMANN, OSCAR. *The Early Church.* Westminster, 1956.
DEDIETRICH, SUZANNE. *The Witnessing Community.* Westminster, 1958.
EDGE, FINDLEY B. *The Church on Fire.* Word, 1972.
JONES, E. STANLEY. *The Reconstruction of the Church.* Abingdon, 1970.

KUNG, HANS. *The Church.* Sheed and Ward, 1967.
LADD, GEORGE ELDON. *Jesus and the Kingdom.* Word, 1964.
O'CONNOR, ELIZABETH. *Call to Commitment.* Harper & Row, 1963.
PHILLIPS, J. B. *New Testament Christianity.* Macmillan, 1956.
THIELICKE, HELMUT. *The Trouble with the Church.* Harper & Row, 1965.
TRUEBLOOD, ELTON. *The Company of the Committed.* Harper & Row, 1961.
———. *The Incendiary Fellowship.* Harper & Row, 1967.

Books on the Corinthian Church

BAIRD, WILLIAM. *The Corinthian Church: A Biblical Approach to Urban Culture.* Abingdon, 1964.
BARCLAY, WILLIAM. *The Letters to the Corinthians.* Westminster, 1954.
BARRETT, C. K. *The First Epistle to the Corinthians.* Harper & Row, 1968.
GLEN, J. STANLEY. *Pastoral Problems in First Corinthians.* Westminster, 1964.

Psychological Helps

HORNEY, KAREN. *Neurosis and Human Growth.* Routledge & Kegan Paul, Ltd., London, 1951.
KUNKEL, FRITZ. *Creation Continues* (on Matthew). Scribner, 1947.
MAVIS, W. CURRY. *The Psychology of Christian Experience.* Zondervan, 1963.
TOURNIER, PAUL. *The Person Reborn.* Harper & Row, 1966.
WHITE, ERNEST. *Christian Life and the Unconscious.* Harper & Row, 1955.

Books on Christian Experience

BONHOEFFER, DIETRICH. *The Cost of Discipleship.* Macmillan, 1937.
CASSELS, LOUIS. *The Reality of God.* Herald Press, 1972.
FERRE, NELS F. S. *Strengthening the Spiritual Life.* Harper & Row, 1951.
JONES, E. STANLEY. *Abundant Living.* Abingdon, 1942.
KELLY, THOMAS R. *A Testament of Devotion.* Harper & Row, 1941.

LOOMIS, EARL A. *The Self in Pilgrimage.* Harper & Row, 1960.

MILLER, KEITH. *A Second Touch.* Word, 1967.

PRICE, EUGENIA. *Just As I Am.* Lippincott, 1968.

_____. *No Pat Answers.* Zondervan, 1972.

✳ RIDENOUR, FRITZ, ED. *How to Be a Christian Without Being Religious.* Regal Books, 1967.

SHOEMAKER, SAM. *Extraordinary Living for Ordinary Men.* Zondervan, 1965.

SMITH, HANNAH WHITEHALL. *My Spiritual Autobiography.* Revell, 1903.

_____. *The Christian's Secret of a Happy Life.* Revell, 1968.

STEERE, DOUGLAS V. *On Beginning from Within.* Harper & Row, 1943.

STEWART, JAMES S. *The Wind of the Spirit.* Abingdon, 1969.

THIELICKE, HELMUT. *The Waiting Father.* Harper & Row, 1959.

TRUEBLOOD, ELTON. *The New Man for Our Time.* Harper & Row, 1970.

WEBB, LANCE. *Discovering Love.* Abingdon, 1959.

73 74 75 76 77 10 9 8 7 6 5 4 3 2 1